THE BODY OF GOD

THE BODY OF GOD

First Steps Toward an Anti-Theology

The Collected Papers of
ERIC GUTKIND

Edited by LUCIE B. GUTKIND and HENRY LE ROY FINCH

Introduction by HENRY LE ROY FINCH

HORIZON PRESS   NEW YORK

Contents

Introduction

It is difficult, if not impossible, to find a single term to describe Eric Gutkind. Words like "poet," "mystic" and "visionary" are one-sided and misleading and do not do justice to the hard intellectual core of his thinking and to his life-long concern with science and mathematics. The word "philosopher" often suggests an abstract universalism which is far removed from the concrete, specific and intuitive nature of his mind. On the other side "religious thinker" is too narrow for one who questioned the very term "religion" and who believed that virtually all our religious language is obsolete and even harmful.

To "place" Eric Gutkind we have to think of such men as Nietzsche, Kierkegaard, Boehme and William Blake. It is the combination of concreteness and immediacy with far-seeingness of vision which defines his special gift. His words startle us repeatedly by their simplicity; they have the obviousness of truth too clear to be seen, and yet, once seen, so natural and evident that we cannot understand how it could have been overlooked. They move in an atmosphere of sanity, healing in its freedom and wholeness.

It is not possible to compartmentalize such a thinker. And it was central to Eric Gutkind's point of view that he rejected all such compartmentalizations in favor of the integral nature of thinking when it arises as genuine speech from the innermost sources of questioning and understanding. Thinking in this sense is the supreme human activity, intrinsically unifying and renewing, the sublation of feeling and passion into vision, uncircumscribed and undivided against itself. Free from anxiety for results, refusing to dictate to or hinder the processes of illumination, never turning its back on the world, it aims to understand just what is most common and ordinary. For it takes this kind of thinking to show us that it is just this world, the world in its full concreteness, which we have not yet reached.

Although he spoke most often, especially in later years, in the idiom of Jewish thought, Gutkind's outlook was universalistic. And although he made use of very ancient ideas, it was always with reference to the future. The most advanced themes of this century—the discovery of the body, the primacy of language, the significance of cybernetics and technology, the meaning of anti-religion and anti-politics, the overcoming of alienation—these were given a far-reaching meaning. The key-note was the revolutionary character of the rejection of idols—nations, races, myths, ideologies, property, prestige. This erstwhile declaration of radicalism acquired a new immediacy because it was linked to an understanding of the forces of science, society and culture which are moving toward the disintegration of the traditional cultural and social fabric.

Gutkind's vision embraced in an inner unity (what for many it seems almost impossible to bring together) the most "existential" and the most "abstract" aspects of modern thought. He saw an essential relatedness between a deepened and purified Marxism, an emphasis on "body theology" and on the physiological aspects of religion, contemporary language philosophy in its various forms and the ever-rising levels of abstraction of modern science and logic. Science and religion, if properly understood, were in his view deeply harmonious. It was for him one and the same movement which detaches us from the world and brings us into the presence of the world.

Religion appeared in Gutkind's work as a "true materialism." He believed that only by looking ever deeper into the material world can we begin to discern the outlines of a higher world. His kinship with such men as Blake, D. H. Lawrence and V. V. Rozanov is evident in his emphasis on the human body and the need to understand the "language of the body" and the "holiness of the body." (Pragmatism, he says in his *Notebooks*, "is not fundamental because it is not physiological.") This is not in conflict with the "primacy of language" and "speech thinking" (ideas showing the influence of Wittgenstein and also of such philosophers as J. G. Hamann) because he also saw a constant reciprocal relation at a profound level between language and body. In the social realm Gutkind saw in Marx the dissolution of ontology into social words and social categories and in modern science the dissolution of the inorganic world of nature into mathematical language. All this pointed to the emergence of a new world-understanding beyond the confines of the traditional body-mind dualism, "ontologized" social fictions and age-old submission to "nature."

The development of Eric Gutkind's thought parallels in an interesting way the development of the thought of his friend the literary and social critic Walter Benjamin (1892-1940). Like Benjamin, Gutkind developed a specifically religious understanding of Marxism, and, also like Benjamin, he was influenced in this by their mutual friend Gershom Scholem (1896-), the historian of Jewish mysticism. The Kabbalistic and Hassidic conception of things as "divine signs" provided the framework for a wider understanding of the Marxist conception of the perversion of things into commodities or social fictions. (The Kantian thing-in-itself could be understood as the last line between this and the realization that "things" are in some fundamental way *words*, a realization brought still nearer by language philosophy and by the cybernetic conception of "information.") While Benjamin went on to show how this perversion of "things" was reflected in various literary and social movements, Gutkind went on to formulate a still broader point of view. His Marxism was integrated into a profound conception that man must be freed, not only from "things" ("Things," he said are *intrinsically* merchandise; the very conception of the "thing" or the "in-itself" is responsible), but also from "power" (a magical idea) and from "images" (linked to mythical thinking). The domination of "things," "powers" and "images" represented a fundamental failure connected with the failure to realize (what Kant's philosophy had indicated) that the world is at bottom, quite literally, an ethical or action phenomenon, and not what classical modern science with its fundamental conception of *energy* had supposed, a mechanical or work phenomenon. With the dismissal of the thing-in-itself must go the further recognition that we do not need either the conception of "power" or "force" or the conception of sense experience regarded as "pictures" in order to understand the world. (Heinrich Hertz's dismissal of "force" from mechanics—which Wittgenstein appropriated in his early philosophy—and Einstein's substitution of geometrical curvature for gravitational "force" are both examples in science of this possibility of dispensing with "forces.")

What distinguished Gutkind, not only from Walter Benjamin, but from other contemporaries in their circle, including Martin Buber and Scholem himself, was Gutkind's continuing concern with science and logic. It is not without significance that his closest personal friend over almost an entire lifetime was the Dutch mathematician L. E. J. Brouwer (1881-1967), certainly one of the great figures in 20th Century mathematics. In the mathematics of Brouwer and in the appplication of mathematics to the physical world by Einstein, Weyl, Dirac and others Gutkind found the confirmation of the view that "no picture covers a reality" and that nature is to be understood solely in terms of abstract mathematical patterns. This he characterized as a liberation from mythology, exploding the "cosmological substratum" as Marx had exploded the "social substratum" and Freud the "psychological substratum."

Still more basic than all these elements in Eric Gutkind's thought, however, was another element, in a sense antedating all the others, an element *sui generis*, at once deeply personal and wholly impersonal, an element which provided the focus for all the rest. This was his experience that "the ego must die" and that this is the crucial meaning of the present historical moment. *"I am not* is a more profound beginning than *I am,"* he said. Thinking, he believed, is the only authentic power in the universe, but it is a power which does not belong to a self, any more than language does. The moment is here when it will not longer be possible to build either life or understanding on the basis of ego-assertion, whether this be individual or collective. (Man cannot be "property," even the "property" of himself, or of nations, races or classes.) The old "realities" of the person, the nation, the race, the class are ineluctably drawing to their ends. The new man will have to submit to the "storm of the spirit" without the protection of ego-identity or collective identifications, which in every respect now threaten to exterminate him. It was Gutkind's conviction that we are on the verge of just this kind of a total transformation, since nothing else will solve the innumerable suicidal problems of our time, which have now been rolled up into one gigantic question—the continued existence of the human race itself. The age-old divided self will have to disappear, not on behalf of an original pantheistic oneness of the Orient (which is only the matrix of history, not its goal), but on behalf of a free journeying of the body-spirit in perpetual self-transcendence. Far from being the negation of individuality, this is its full realization.

This theme was announced with an apocalyptic urgency and an eloquence which reminded many people of Nietzsche in Gutkind's first book *Siderische Geburt* (*Sidereal Birth*) published in 1910. The catastrophes which befell the world in two World Wars and befell the Jews under the Nazis did nothing to shake this conviction, but, on the contrary, reinforced his view that the world is going through its "noon-tide terror," when all that was previously thought to be sufficient is seen to be insufficient. He believed that if we do not wish to suffocate in a world grown too small or be destroyed by our own frustration in such a world, we will have to break out into something wholly new. Only the abandonment of the ego-self, *dictated as it is now by sheer necessity*, can bring about the change.

This aspect of Gutkind's experience brought him into relation with another prophetic figure—Dimitrije Mitrinovic (1887-1953), whose influence was strongly felt in British intellectual circles between the two World Wars. Mitrinovic was a Serbian from Herzegovina who played an important role in the intellectual and literary ferment which led to the creation of modern Yugoslavia. He studied in various European universities and migrated to London in 1914, where he remained until his death. Mitrinovic may be described as a Christian theosophist, strongly influenced by the Russian philosopher Vladimir Soloviev and teaching a pan-Europeanism as an essential ingredient in the spiritual unity of mankind, a unity which provided a transcendent "mission" for each nation as well as for science and the secular development. His powerful personality and remarkable gifts of insight into human beings made him a dominating (and even in some respects awesome) figure in a number of groups. Words such as "uncanny" and "hypnotic" were often applied to Mitrinovic. (For example by Paul Selver in his book on *Orage and the "New Age" Circle* (1959). Selver describes his first meeting with Mitrinovic this way: "Hardly had I shaken hands with Mitrinovic than I found myself so affected by his mere presence that I nearly lost consciousness. This had never before happened to me, nor did it ever happen again.")

Mitrinovic was introduced to Gutkind by the painter Wassily Kandinsky before the First World War. The two men established an instant rapport. Sharing Gutkind's vision of the new age, Mitrinovic made *Siderische Geburt* the platform of his New Europe Group and of the magazine *New Albion* whch he edited with A. R. Orage in 1934. Orage had previously published writings by Mitrinovic under the pseudonym of "M. M. Cosmoi" before becoming involved with the teaching of G. I. Gurdjieff and abandoning his literary activities to work with Gurdjieff at Fontainebleau in France.

Both Mitrinovic and Gutkind were men of genius, but Mitrinovic's genius lay in direct dealings with people, while Gutkind's was expressed in ideas and writing. What they shared was that in both of them the ordinary concerns of the self had been replaced by a new intensity of vision (as much, it seemed to many, physiological as psychological). The self-security and self-enhancement (which consciously and unconsciously determine the lives of most men) had been transformed in them into a clairvoyant kind of "seeing." What Gutkind said of Mitrinovic could have been said of him also: "He was so incomparably present; and often all the others seemed to be less real, to be less present."

Eric Gutkind, as the years went by, ceased to use the word *I* either in lectures or in conversation. Although his thinking was nothing if not "existential," what was merely personal ceased to be important. He would, it is certain, have objected to biographical facts being included in an introduction to his writings. The only justification for them here is that they may help in some way toward an understanding of his ideas.

He was born in 1877 of a wealthy family in Berlin, the son of a manufacturer, his mother's family descended from the poet Heine. When he was 12 or 13 his family hired as a tutor for him the Kantian philosopher Paul Apel, then a young man, later known as the author of *Geist und Materie* (1905) and *Die Ueberwindung des Materialismus* (1909). (It is said that the family became worried when the small boy walked around the house pondering such truths as "reality contradicts itself.") Apel gave Gutkind a lasting admiration for Kant and a desire to solve the riddle of the thing-in-itself (a solution which only began to emerge later when he discovered Boehme, Schelling, Hegel and Marx).

At the University of Berlin Gutkind studied with the anthropologist Adolph Bastian (1826-1905), whom he later described as the last man able to speak most known languages. His studies were primarily in art history, philosophy, psychology and religion, but science remained important, and he was active as an amateur astronomer. He and his wife Lucie Baron, whom he married in 1910, traveled widely in Europe and the Middle East.

The success of his first book *Siderische Geburt* served to widen the circle of his friends. It brought him into contact with the Dutch educator and writer Frederik van Eeden (1860-1932), and together they formed a group which met in Berlin and at the Gutkind summer home in Potsdam. This group included Walter Rathenau (1867-1922), the political leader later assassinated; Brouwer, the mathematician; Florens Christian Rang (1864-1924), the theologian and historian; Henri Borel (1869-1933), the Orientalist; Gustav Landauer (1870-1919), the left-wing leader; and Martin Buber (1878-1963), the theologian. These were joined at various times by Walter Benjamin and by the American Upton Sinclair.

Siderische Geburt in its style and expression belongs in the tradition of German romanticism. It shows the influence of Novalis,

Schelling, Boehme and Nietzsche, as well as of the highly influential German poet Stefan George. It is a hymnodic rhapsody to a new age, written with little attention to organization or system, but with an exuberance of poetic imagery. Its apocalyptic theme is expressed in terms more Gnostic and Christian than Jewish. It links the coming age "beyond the self" to the development of philosophy and science, which are leading to the "death of the world" and the "birth of the deed."

During the 1920's, influenced by Scholem and others, Gutkind moved toward a radical reinterpretation of traditional Judaism, more advanced and daring than that of Martin Buber or of their other Jewish philosophical contemporary Franz Rosenzweig (1886-1929). But while Buber's ideas, and to a lesser extent Rosenzweig's, have been largely absorbed into present-day religious discourse, Gutkind's have still to be discovered. It is predictable that in time Gutkind, the last of this triumvirate to be recognized, may well appear as the most significant of the three.

Although Gutkind belonged to no organizations, his open opposition to the Nazis in lectures and articles made him a marked man, and in 1933 he and his wife escaped from Germany on a few hours' notice. (Attempts to save his mother and other relatives failed, and they died a few years later in concentration camps.) He lived in London for part of the year 1933, and there was published the English translation of his second book *The Absolute Collective*.

In a bare hundred pages of the most highly charged (and yet at the same time austere and even astringent) prose this remarkable document, with the subtitle *A Philosophical Attempt to Overcome Our Broken State*, sets forth Gutkind's mature vision. With a kind of burning intensity, compacted like a laser beam, it qualifies as a genuine prophetic utterance, itself an expression of its own definition of Man as "absolute speech." In its extreme condensation, in which sentences of deceptive simplicity bear an enormous weight of meaning, as well as in its apodictic and enunciatory style, it is quite beyond anything which is ordinarily called a *book*. No concessions are made, no explanations are given;

the demand on the reader is not to read, but to live with it and slowly to find his way into it.

The Absolute Collective established itself among a small but widening circle. Among its most enthusiastic proponents was the American writer Henry Miller, who in an essay about it published in 1941, described it as a book "born at precisely the right time," a book inspired by "a deep certitude" which creates "a residue of truth which is implicit and unshakable." Miller became one of Gutkind's admirers and was responsible for bringing him into touch with a number of other American writers and students.

In the Fall of 1933 Gutkind came to the United States and settled in New York City, where he remained until his death in the Summer of 1965. He and his wife became American citizens in 1938. During this period he gave hundreds of lectures, first for many years at the New School, and then at Yeshiva University, the Master Institute of United Arts and in the adult education division of the City College. These lectures ranged from such topics as *New Frontiers in Psychology, Restating the American Dream,* and *The Dilemma of Science and Technology* to *The Wisdom of the Kabbalah, The Jewish Ritual* and *Modern Man* and *Zen vs. Cybernetics.* The last book published during his lifetime came out in 1952 with the title *Choose Life.*

Choose Life is at once the most specifically Jewish and the most accessible of Gutkind's books. Clearly intended to reach a wide audience, it presents an interpretation of Judaism which repudiates liberalism and reformism and finds in the Orthodox tradition the sources for a radical manifesto for the future. It is the expression in Jewish terms of the possibilities of the "liberation of man," linking particularism with universalism and the past with an age still to come.

On his death he left a number of *Notebooks,* several unpublished articles and tape-recorded transcripts of a few of his many lectures. The present volume brings together translations of parts of the *Notebooks,* articles previously unpublished (together with some published in the *Jewish Press* in 1955-56) and excerpts from *Siderische Geburt,* not before available in English. (An unpublished English translation of *Siderische Geburt* was made for the British writer Lady (Victoria) Welby (1837-1912), the correspondent of Charles Peirce and herself the author of a number of books on language. This translation has been drawn upon for the present one.)

The *Notebooks* are of special interest because they contain Gutkind's final reflections and some of his most advanced ideas. They show that right up until the moment of his death he was moving into new territory and applying his interpretation of the Kabbalah ever more radically to the contemporary scene. The *Notebooks* deserve to stand beside *The Absolute Collective* as genuinely prophetic utterances. Especially in what they have to say about ritual, cybernetics, language and the body they foreshadow religious movements which still lie ahead on the other side of the "death of God."

The *Notebooks* are written in the style of disconnected aphorisms, the style in which Gutkind intended to bring out his next book. In their succinctness and completeness each sentence frequently has the force of a kind of philosophical haiku which can stand by itself. Yet each aphorism supports the others and together they express in something like a final form what his writings had always expressed—the "transparency of the world."

In the present tumultuous period Eric Gutkind is especially the philosopher for the young. He has something of the greatest importance to say to the generation which is groping its way beyond liberalism and at the same time beyond ideologies and beyond technology and a narrow pragmatism and "practicalism." In the attempt to find a meaningful existence in the midst of spiritual exhaustion, this generation will find in him a voice wholly positive and wholly present. He speaks for the "only affirmation which will stand"—the affirmation of the unified man, free from the "split in human consciousness" and by the same token free from the dead hand of the past.

Our age is not lacking in those who expose its negativity and emptiness, but there are few who see what lies beyond this. Eric Gutkind's work is a whole-hearted *Yes* to an entirely different future, and this is its deepest secret. It springs, not from a partial diagnosis of what is wrong, but from a total affirmation of an age as-yet-to-be-born. And it is this which enables it to cast a strong light on the present, for only those who are beyond the present can understand the present. The human situation will require, and is moving toward, a clean sweep. It will appear that much, if not everything, is to be lost, and this realization will be painful. But the pain is the pain of growth, and the truth is that nothing which is real is to be lost, and everything is to be gained if we can let go of what is dead or dying.

Eric Gutkind attempted to get to the root of our problems. He described the present age as one of a "great discarding," comparable only to the step which led to the beginning of history itself. We are coming, he said, to the end of what has been called history. And the "discarding" now will be even greater than the "discarding" at the beginning of history. We stand at the other end of the road which led through Lascaux and Altamira—the beginning in the prehistoric caves of the "images," the beginning of the attempt to "grasp" the world in "pictures." This was the start of the decisive human separation from nature. Today as we realize what modern science is telling us—that no pictures of the world are possible any longer—the profound inner division created by the pictures begins to come to an end. This is the true "farewell to Mother Nature" when the umbilical cord is finally cut. As we let go of the "images," we let go also of the notion of "things" (the in-itself) and of the "divided self" (the self-image). For none of these are ultimate realities. Through an inner unification we are born out of "nature" into the ever immanently transcendent "world."

The greatness of man is his capacity for action. True action means action "outside ourselves" from a source of spontaneity greater than ourselves. But, as Gutkind said, our spontaneity is weak; we are formed by events, passions and forces, instead of being the masters of these. "In his present state Man has as his foundation only the passive, the receptive side; and the active, the spontaneous side is merely a kind of super-structure." This was expressed in *Siderische Geburt* in this way: "What does brokenness really mean? It means that the two components of man, the passive and the active, are split apart and then mended in a perverted way. There are two sides to human nature: receptivity and spontaneity. We are passive in our apperception of perceptions. But we are spontaneous in our acts of self-determination. These two aspects form a unity like the circulation of the blood through veins and arteries. We cannot exist without receptivity, and we cannot continue to be human beings without our spontaneous and free activity. But our spontaneity must take the lead and our receptivity must be led. Receptivity must be subordinated; such is the primal image of Man; such is the real significance of Man."

Does this, as it may seem if not properly understood, promise only an age of anarchic impulse and futile drifting on the other side of history? Only if we suppose that the action of the unified human being does not have its own *raison d'etre* within itself and that the motivation for all action must lie with the divided self. For if the illusory self-image has been the erstwhile historical mainspring of action (as much in one part of the world as in another), the time when this is either logically or psychologically or socially possible is fast drawing to a close. The murderous urge which draws its sustenance from a lack of wholeness too profound to be satisfied by any achievement and which requires perpetual self-justification through the denial of others, reaches its natural culmination in the suicidal facts of modern war. It is what we are afraid to lose, which in fact we have never "possessed," which threatens our extinction.

The special dilemma of today is that a mere opposition to any fundamental aspects of this situation only sets up a polarization which remains entirely within the old framework. The divided self cannot oppose the divided self, any more than (as Marx saw) an ordinary class can oppose the principle of classes or a nation the principle of nations. When something has to be left behind, the process is more like the snake sloughing off its skin, or a dreamer awakening from his dreams than it is like a counterforce pushing against something until it gives way. If the very terms of the understanding are not changed, nothing is changed; and this change itself *is* the change. Gutkind repeatedly spoke of the need to *outgrow* the past, for he saw that there will be, and inevitably must be, resistance to change which does not really change, while true change "happens" while, as it were, we are looking the other way.

The schizophrenia of the human being, accepted as "normal," perverts both a genuine individualism and a genuine collectivism. The Cartesian fallacy which confuses the imaginary locked-away self with the genuine individual is balanced by the Leninist fallacy which supposes that it is possible to "organize" Communism. And both social directions are victims of the delusion that it is technology and the "technical approach" which is the answer to our problems. The truth is, as Gutkind reminded us, that if every technological problem were solved, the ultimate problems of mankind would still not be touched at all.

Our age is destined to learn a lesson about the radical limitations of technological abundance. However much such abundance is to be desired, it offers no psychological or spiritual abundance. The latter continues to elude us just because it cannot be "possessed" or "organized" or "controlled" or "used." It is just what we *are* and springs only from the aboriginal freedom and spontaneity of the human being. There is nothing which we can "have," least of all ourselves, which can substitute for what we fail to "be." And there is not, and never will be, any "way" to our freedom, since freedom is itself the way.

Once this is fully realized and *seen* in all of its ramifications (so that no escape from it is possible any longer), then what lies ahead is a new freedom and unity of the human being for whom action arises not from any lack, but from the fulness which goes with inner unification and freedom. The long "postponement of history" is over, and a new level of human existence begins. These words have the ring of something "ideal" or "utopian," especially when thought of in social terms, and it is difficult to realize that they describe something very close and perhaps never before so close. The human race has undergone catastrophic changes in its long course, including "mutations of consciousness." Anyone who thinks at all deeply about the present situation must know that it is on the verge of another one. We are indeed "outgrowing the world," and it is the orientation of tens of thousands of years which is no longer adequate. We are not at liberty now to *try* the final alternative, or by some effort of self-will to select it or impose it. We will find ourselves *there* (where in a sense we have always been) by the easiest of steps when all else is ready.

Despite the darkness of the hour (and our age is destined to suffer as no previous age ever has) something very old and yet totally new, fully sufficient for our problems, is near at hand. It is evident with the greatest simplicity and intensity in the writings of Eric Gutkind, as well as in other places. It involves in the end, not a saying *no*, but only the act of seeing ever more clearly and deeply, the act which embraces the whole world and slowly and effortlessly lifts it up into its true meaning.

Henry LeRoy Finch
Sarah Lawrence College
September, 1968

Notebooks / 1958-1965

The Tent

What is needed now:
Undo the doing = the setting free of man.
Unshell the shells = ending the domination of nature.
Unsplit the split = healing the primal break.

Nature has failed and must be relegated to its rightful place.	Man has failed and must be elevated to rituality, the one way open.

What is owned will decay. The end of all "in-itselfness."

From dichotomy to trichotomy is the step beyond the primal schizophrenia. New dimensions must be added or suffocation will ensue; new words as names for new orders.

The Midst of the People is not a locality. It is trans- or super-topological. There HE "emerges" and does not merely "exist." No theology, rather *presentness* or *non-presentness*. We can reach the Midst. All else only "follows" from it.

Nothing but the ritual unification is incandescent enough to achieve the community that does not dissolve into uniformity, does not fuse or organize but rather elevates to genuine unity. The smallest step of the few toward this genuine unity would be the "Great Step of Today," the "Wonder of Today." Any affiliations are superficial by contrast with the depths of this ritual transformation, which means transcending and not levelling.

Genuine unifications are non-additive and far stronger than any mysticism. Those who journey towards the Midst can achieve oneness.

Images split	*Powers murder*	*Things rob*
Three Depths	*Three Nothings*	*Three Splits*
Matrix	Images	Primal Split (*Kizzutz*)
Masses	Powers	Breaking-up (*Shevirah*)
Matter	Things	Letting-free (*Zimzum*)

Ritual is anti-pictorial, a sovereignty over pictures.

The cosmos—taken as nature—is silent now. Nature is exhausted. Original Man (*Adam Kadmon*) failed, the original shells (*kelim*) of nature broke, yet Man is still open.

Abraham exclaimed: "Now listen, ye heavens, and I will speak."

Can "things" be false? Yes. Things are not unequivocal.

Hasidic saying: "Only HE is clearly there. Besides HIM nothing is clearly there."

The Messianic movement is now with Marx and not with Jesus.

No rising higher if not aimed at speaking.

The fear of meeting HIM is greater than the fear of death.

The mystic does not "meet"; he submerges.

"Existence" is not the last word. The ring of death—the images, the powers, the things—can be thrown off.

The Midst of the People is attainable, nothing else is.

Theology is impossible. Ritual is possible.

The cosmos is delegated to us, and only this "delegated cosmos" is comprehensible, but it has not yet been accepted.

The spirit of capitalism, in whatever form, is the absoluteness of "things," the most radical atheism ever formulated. Matter could have a divine meaning were it not perverted into "commodities."

Pragmatism does not function, as generally assumed. It is an abysmal failure. Functioning does not make anything "true." The false also can "function."

Theory is superior to practice. It is primal and creates "positions."

Ritual *meets* HIM, does not *possess* HIM.

Ascending = Holy—(*Kadosh*) = Pure—(*Tahor*)
Speaking = Devotion—(*Devekuth*) = Tent—(*Devir*)
Standing upright = Whole—(*Tam*) = Trembling—(*Haredim*)

Man is detachable from the three substructures: cosmology—psychology—economy. This was done by Einstein, Freud and Marx. All three substructures must be externalized and discarded as "pre-outside." The last mighty discarding happened in totemistic times when totemism discarded the identity with the animal and made the animal the ancestor. But matrix without patrix is demonic. A supernal connection is not merely a "superstructure."

Discardings today:

The pragma	The robot	The thing
penetrable	detachable	suspendable

Discarded but not yet ritualized
What is the common note in Marx, Freud, Einstein? It is the discarding of the three substructures, the presupposition for man's liberation. Man is not yet Man when still economical, psychological, cosmological. He also cannot be understood as "pragmatic-functional," but only as ritual, which means "being-called-for, directed, delegated."

All "in-itselfness" is utterly false. It is evil and aloof and hence demonic. If "having" is not externalized, it will rot. Embracement is not "havable." HE listens and speaks to the "have-nots" (the *Itarutah*). HE does not speak to the "haves."

The new global masses have a message, a "message of the lowly," an *Itarutah*-message. No longer can they be the shapeless of yesteryear. They will develop a new mentality. There will be an *upward levelling.*

Today an ultimate tearing away from the lower strata is taking place, a connecting to the higher point, where the Ritual begins. The transcending Man is more easily ritualized than the static Man. A new dimension has been added. The single individual is "imploded" towards the real plurality.

As the word is corrupted so is the face. The body now is dumb, and the face is degenerating because both are unritualized. The ritualized, transparent corporeality is no longer known. The human body is not being steered; it is not in a "field."

The Primal Moments Return
Zimzum (letting free)   *Shevirah* (breaking-up)   *Kizzutz* (primal split)

Now HE returns. Already HE reaches the outposts! When HE is in the Midst, a tremendous incandescence will burst forth. Without the Midst nothing is decisive. We can only "transcend" into the Midst. In the Midst is the word, and there HE emerges.

Ethics as an "effort" fails to be trans-magic.

By rituality and "extranity" we can get an attachment to the higher vortices.

Everything now is encompassed by the human element, including physics.

Being seen from the Midst makes "things" no longer thingish. The Biblical bread was always before the Divine Countenance in the midst of the Tent, and this was the guarantee that it was there for all.

Ritual charges, culture discharges. The three "unfinished revolutions" come to perfection in the Ritual.

Just where no one speaks of HIM, just there He appears. "Where the Name is not uttered there the Name is present." (*Lo sh'mo bo sh'mo.*)

From theology to theophany leads over and beyond the crisis of "God is dead."

A radical detachment from all metaphysics today makes the world *here* and *now*. Such a world in all its profundity, delivers us from the embracement of death.

Ritual is rebellion, because it is anti-"doing," the anti-pole to magic and force. Today we are arriving at the melting-point of the fire of the Ritual. "To suspend a mountain on a hair." That exists, today! What is the "hair?" The Ritual! Everything must be suspended from that height after the total discarding of the three-fold raging of economy, psychology, cosmology. They are unmasked, analyzed, relativized! Everything then runs into Man. The three no longer stand alone but are in a "field." By themselves they are pre-human. There is no "nature," "soul," "economy," and no "in-itself."

Religion and social orders cannot hold their ground and are withering away. We are today less confronted with "somethings" than with "nothings."

The Midst is an incandescent melting-point. *There* are the bread, the word and the keys. The Tent is the place of speech. The old theories of language make no sense. Speech is trialistic, not a monologue or dialogue. The third is always present. In our conventional banal speech we witness today, as part of the common emptiness, the destruction of language.

The "priestly hierarchy" (*Hekhaloth*) is not a power structure, but a kind of "information-structure."

Genuine "standing upright" engenders fear and trembling.

Our "doing" is obsolete because it is only a "making." *Now* we are beginning really to "do" at a greater depth. There is a "higher depth" and a "deeper height!"

The world not only "is," but has been "commanded." It cannot be understood from the viewpoint of "existence."

Death is chosen not intrinsic. Life is not yet chosen.

Ontology, radically open and public, is sociology. Sociology as only managerial is demonic, because its focus is not extran. The "extranity" of the world is not a beyond! Communism is not yet "Ritual," and thus so far inadequate.

Conflict is in God, but is delegated to Man that he should give an answer to this Divine conflict. The pattern of "question-answer" reveals the intent to "get out of it," not the decided will to "get into it"—that is, into the profundity of the conflict. Without "being delegated," Man is only functional and pre-human.

The threefold raging of sociology, psychology and cosmology has become itself a virtual ritual, no less strict in its demands than the genuine Ritual.

It should be stressed again and again that Man is confronted now only with himself, so there is absolutely no "an sich" (in-itself).

The Midst is the Midst of the People. All other "midsts" are mere pre-stages.

There is a profound relation of letting-free (*Zimzum*) and Speaking, since genuine speech is not mere defining, nor ontics, nor "somethings."

Holiness (*Kadosh*) means "raised above," "lifted free," and this is Ritual. "Organized" is far from being "ritualized."

Man is the "bound binder," "bound to God" by the prayer straps (*Teffilin*). He is the freedom of the universe, of nature. He can transcend himself.

The Way—The Jump—There!! Suddenness is the hope, rather than evolution.

"Israel" means that HE reigns.

The Ritual must transcend these distortions:
Things into merchandise—holes
Powers into the state—murder
Images into the arts—evasion

The Ritual "charges" the "world-spiral." Nothing else "charges" basically.

The Ritual of sacrifice was a saying NO to the "havable," an act of letting-free (*Zimzum*). The new letting-free (*Zimzum*), the new breaking up (*Shevirah*), the new primal choice (*Kizzutz*) is the true demarcation line.

All genuine radical rebellion originates in HIM—a Divine bolshevism. (Bolshoi—literally not a political term, means "maximal.")

A paramount conflict: the mutual destruction of substructure and superstructure, demasking and dissolving.

Sickness is not natural; it is a ritualistic failure. Sickness is not intrinsic; it is acquired.

The increase of reality is not simply given, but the culmination of a profound Ritual. Real additivity is physical, though not natural. It is a change brought about by the Ritual in the attempt to reach the highest heights immediately. Everything—World and Man—originates in the letting-free (*Zimzum*), not out of ontics. Ontic explanations are totally devoid of truth. The human body, if pure, is a ritual result; otherwise it could not be at all.

Where is the precise point to kindle anew the fire of the Ritual? This fire must be hot enough—and nothing else is hot enough —to bring about the melting into a "real unity," which is fundamental, not a resultant. Real multiplicity is not an aggregate, not a given addition or sum. The great new step is the letting-free (*Zimzum*) of Man!

Theology is extreme atheism, because in theology the one who "exists" is subordinated to existence, thus idolatrizing "existence." Existence does not exist, but suspends itself dialectically. "Beyond" is replaced by "extranity," but an extranity of this world, with the Midst and the Indweller. Focus this world here. The Midst of the People, not causality, is primal.

The Ritual brings back the origin and the greatest opportunity in confronting us again with the letting-free (*Zimzum*), the breaking-up (*Shevirah*) and the primal choice (*Kizzutz*).

Body is not private; it is never without "people." Man without People has a cadaver only. Body must be understood as the *Mysterium Maximum*. The ultimate human body and God is the maximal synthesis. Each individual may become "total," reaching that capacity, which is *the* total capacity.

The Sabbath is a breaking-off, an interrupting, not merely a rest.

We reach the body, a colossal change! We emerge from pre-existence.

A quasi-cybernetic language: The machine is not a "machine," Body is not "body." God is not "God."

Time is cumulative, not "linear" or "spatial." It has several dimensions. If we do not see this, there is "time-horror."

All spheres, seen by God, are only "material." This is "absolute materialism."

The Ritual is a raising of all our faculties to the maximum and enables us to live with maximal intensity. The dammed-up and collected physical strength of the People is almost limitless. It focuses the Midst.

In genuine communism HE would emerge. The fear Man has is the fear of HIS emerging.

Speaking must ascend and ascending must speak!

Nature is not primal; it is pre-human, pre-historic, pre-ritual.

In the superstructure are no ultimates but symptoms.

From *Corruption* to *Purification*
From *Evasion* to *Intensification*
From *Confusion* to *Clarification*

Our supreme task: To arrive at a genuine unity, the only road to becoming *a People with a Midst*. No organization or mystical unity can achieve this.

Not "I and Thou" but *trialism*. "I and Thou" is still dichotomy. But Speaking is *trichotomy* because the Third is in it. Two never meet, never speak, never hear.

The Bible is not religious but ritualistic. Religious interpretations are wrong, even anti-Biblical. The Bible is concerned with the obvious, the concrete, yet as "seen" by God. The Bible leaves nature behind. The phenomena are "signals of the Ritual," an accumulation of the primal origins in the ritual melting-fire, a pre-biology. There is no melting in the superstructure, only empty unities. No genuine unity is possible on a lower stage than the People. The People's unity is without levelling.

He never is alone, HE always is *Makom* (Place).

People is directed against nature. It is trans-natural, also trans-cosmological and trans-economical. We do not yet think in terms of People, that is, in trialistic terms.

Turning to Death closes, turning to Ritual opens up. Finiteness can be pure.

What is the "new body," the "bodily body," the "*Shiur* body"? It is not anti-body, but *body as such*. This is the great divide between two immensely different conceptions of the body, *antis* and *shiurs*.

Epistemology operates with the conception of the closed subject.

The subject is open ritualistically; only functionally is it a closed "within." Man is open, and therefore no epistemology is needed. Since Kant epistemology becomes an ethical problem.

Acting or doing out of unbrokenness is hardly known yet. Who acts? Who is doing? The *split* person. A non-split acting, a non-split doing goes with the Ritual.

The arts substitute for Ritual. This is utterly wrong. Ritual should substitute for the arts. "Abstract" is "concrete," because without images. What is concrete can be addressed. Not so the spook of images.

Saadya's Three: (1) Creation out of nothing (*Yesh me ayin*) points to the relativity of nature. (2) God's relation to each one is immediate with no intermediaries. (3) Justice here, not in the hereafter; a social radicalism.

The Ritual is an experience of unification. Only the Ritual can overtake the raging technique and reduce it to its proper proportions. No "organizing" can do this.

Israel as a people, rather than a nation or a power-system, means "sanity."

Not the "spiritual," the forever remote, but the Now-and-Here, undiluted.

God "an sich" is a contradiction in itself, profoundly unethical. All "in itself" is profoundly unethical. The Whole (*Tam*), unbroken and unsplit, replaces the "is."

Below us now is the robot. Mere inert factuality is robotic and must be discarded. The totemistic revolution, still unfinished, dealt with the animal.

Man, like a torsionist, is turning himself around now into "extranity." He is turning himself out of all loneliness, all evolution, all ontics, all "an sichs" and all mere functioning into the Ritual. Man, created out of nothing, cannot aim at "something," and is not directed toward "something." Man's torsion is a higher rotation.

Because of the total letting-free (*Zimzum*) the death-ring has been shattered (images, powers, things). The Ritual affects our psychophysiological constitution, which is our deepest tie with the universe. Death is not a physiological, but a ritualistic and ethical problem.

The Ritual overtakes the biological. The time-honored natural body no longer suffices. Our capacities are so great that they tear apart the old narrowness of nature. Nature is perverted; it has failed as a basis. Nevertheless our body is still a merely natural body, coming from nature. Nature cannot go further. The Ritual component is still covered-up.

Yet, the Ritual can overtake nature and penetrate into the biostructure of the body. The body can be changed as we reach the pre-biological and the pre-physiological. Because HE is body we can attain a new body, which no longer is a death-like inferior body, but wholly Divine. HIS BODY is an unheard-of tremendous new conception.

No intermediaries, no "in betweens," only immediacy! HE—and no messenger!

Spinoza—Philo—Jesus—three wayward Jews.

Nature now is relativized, the soul analyzed, economy de-ontologized. Nature is pushed back and reaches an end, the soul is pushed outside or "extranized," and economy is turned upside down from basis to consequence.

The more abstract is also the more concrete because *pictures alienate*. Thinking is mute, silent, but it should speak. Thinking that hears, speaks. Because abstract thinking is picture-free, it can be *speech-thought*.

HE is present as the Name, not as power. HE is not ontic, but semantic, a speech-phenomenon of tremendous magnitude. HE calls.

Our "Today" is empty, absent, impure and immoral. Nothing is really present. Everything is only *per se*, alone, private, or "has itself."

The organic, with suddenness like an explosion, forms itself, and this is Ritual. In Ritual the body builds itself. Instantly—right away —suddenly . . . profoundly Jewish.

Three: Relativity—Extranity—Rituality.

Pragmatism does not "fear and tremble," ergo: it does not "stand upright," is not "verticalized."

Mastering of the emotions is one of the foremost consequences of the Ritual. He who has not mastered his emotions still is pre-ritualistic. Ritual changes body and therefore also the structures of the emotions, transforming them into fuel for the fire and hence no longer a danger.

A trans-historical breaking-off: The founding of a People, a genuine People. HE needs Man, a People, that HE may dwell in their Midst.

The Ritual regulates the relation between People and the Midst. The Camp, as an act brought about by the Midst, cannot break up.

Horizontal lines—not only ancestral lineage.

The real multiplicity is not ideological or additive. It has a Midst of enormous might, transcending all of nature. To that point where the keys are, only the Ritual can reach. Nothing else can. Ritual ultimately is totally trans-natural.

A "genuine People" means having risen higher. A step toward this —were it ever so small—would be a definite beginning. On the level of "normalcy" no real change is possible! Man is enveloped in higher dimensions. A People creates "presence," transforming infinity into finiteness.

The sanctification of the World is Biblical. What the religions say is not Biblical. They are fast losing their binding-power and are becoming merchandise.

Already in the Psalms there is a lowering, a giving-up of the Biblical, replacing it by a more "realistic" wordly view.

The World is on the verge of emerging, it is not yet concrete. The more HE is present within it, the more concrete it will be. We are coming to the point where the let-free *Zimzum*-world replaces the split *Kizzutz*-world, and the let-free *Zimzum*-Man replaces the split *Kizzutz*-Man.

Where HE lives there is Reality.

Speaking is addressing. Addressing is praying. Spinoza's repudiation of this is wrong. Speaking is not defining. Speaking is this mysterious entering into a new Here, a new Now, a new Suddenness. One cannot talk *to* God.

There is not yet body, or soul, or meeting, or speech.

"Extranity" in Gödel's mathematics. Nothing can be explained "out-of-itself." Everything is in an "orbit."

Ritual unmasks "doing" as the computer unmasks the robot in Man and also unmasks logic as still imbued with mechanics and hence sub-logical. Our doing is still robotic, magical.

Where the "nisus" (upsurge of nature) closes there Man opens.

"Body" means complete openness.

"Letting-free" in the profoundest sense has nothing to do with theology. It means that nothing is idolatrized, and there HE emerges. It is not a something, an *in-itself* or an aloneness. It is nearness, minus the "ring of death." HIS emerging is not theology, or pantheism, but "The Name Here" (*bo sh'mo*).

Call—call upon—call forth—call away!

Life is no epiphenomenon. Life is primal and inherent in the world. World is no epiphenomenon, or resultant.

The "grey substance" in the brain is the evolutionary "homonization." It is neither causal nor final, but another dimension.

Dissolutions: Marx . . . Father (ruler)
Freud . . . Birth (origins)
Einstein . . . Mother (nature)

Autonomy means irreducibility. It completely shuts out the strata below.

Revolution is a bending downward, an inclining. Ritual is an ascending, penetrating into the higher envelopes (*Hekhaloth*).

Man is theomorph, *not* God is anthropomorph.

To speak downwards is merely to dominate. To speak upward is to call, to hear, to open up, to pray.

Capitalism is organized irreality, an established emptiness.

Pragmatic "doing" is managerial, functional. Ritual "doing" is being steered, lifted higher.

What is evil in the "to be" as such? That it is not yet a letting-free (*Zimzum*), but a murderous split (*Kizzutz*).

God eliminates "God." All ontics are removed from the Divine Demand.

Said the rabbi of Worki: "Dance motionless—kneel standing—cry out silent."

Cybernetics is leading us toward the Third, a trans-dichotomy. We can jump over our own shadow.

From the prototype of Man (*Adam Kadmon*) to fainted Man (*Adam Enosh*). Then history, from Man trembling before God (*Haredim*) to Man also the friend of God (*Yedidyah*).

The absolute "in-itself" (*Ding an sich*) is profoundly idolatrous.

Judaism has no ontologies, but it "hears and does not remain silent."

The place of sacrifice (*Ko*) as polar, an above and below. Have these two boundaries been reached today?

Against Spinoza: All metaphysical conceptions, e.g. substance or first cause, have no religious meaning whatsoever.

The let-free (*Zimzum*) of God is the deepest root of all conflicts. This root is not in the "isness," but in the "focusing" (*emzaic*).

The second *Kizzutz* unveils the split. The second *Shevirah* establishes relativity. The second letting-free (*Zimzum*) is the letting-free (*Zimzum*) of Man.

Our focus is extran, that is, ritualistic and not functional.

Shifting the accent from superstructure to the Midst.

Ritual brings back the "Three Primals"—*Zimzum, Shevirah, Kizzutz. We can get to these keys.*

Ritual is super-technology. Not merely the physical but also the biological is affected. It is a steering of biological or organic change.

A far profounder unity than in all groups, races, nations and religions is the "primal unity." This unitedness is extremely strong. The real multiplicity comes only with the unity of the People and God in their Midst.

A task is delegated to Man, which only he can accomplish: to proclaim the Word.

Purity is ultimate, pragma is not. Pragma is secondary. Pragmatics must be circum-ritualized or steered.

Away with all ontics, cosmics, psychics, and into the real multiplicity! The deepest depth is accessible to us.

Ritual is a dangerously great truth. (This is my "$e = m c^2$")

Death is impurity (*Tumah*), a Ritual-failure, not physiological. The shallowness of "explaining" death!

When ritual mistakes are not taken as unessential, but as endangering human life, only then do we have a genuine Ritual.

Ritual as the summation of all organic powers. The "nisus" can reach up to the Ritual. Ritual purity is fundamental. Nature is enveloped by Man. Ritual replaces nature. Ritual is a "doing" in HIS Presence.

A fundamental change: When the *Kizzutz*-phenomena have come to an end!

Communism is not yet "verticalized"; it still lacks the higher dimensions.

Nothing practical or functional can reach the point where the condensed dammed-up strength of a People lies.

The "Now" is looked at today mostly from an outmoded viewpoint that is too reductive, too inorganic. The organic slides downwards then and is lost again. This must be changed.

God is finite and therefore concrete.

There is a primal conflict, yes, but all conflicts are delegated to Man and are our conflicts now.

"Outside" is not outside of the world, but in the midst of the world. The Midst is an externality. God—Man—World are outside themselves.

Ritual becomes obsolete if looked at as a "making" or a "pragma," but it becomes incredibly forward-directed and new as the letting-free (*Zimzum*) of Man.

The New Theophany is in the word, in speaking and in the body. No more cosmic fireworks!

The body unritualized is dumb and stupid and remains unredeemed. The problem is that Ritual and body in their fullest depth do not emerge if HIS Body (*Shiur Komah*) is not accepted. If it were accepted, the human body would become radiant.

Communism ritualized is People. People replaces theology.

The "outsidedness" is not yet clearly recognized.

Two Deaths: Finiteness (*Maveth*) plus-Zero. Perdition (*Avadon*) minus-Zero.

Christianity, like the ants, poetry and pictures, is an evading. No Messiah has come—so far

NOW!

We are striding out of ourselves.
We are approaching the Midst.
We are leaving the superstructures.
We are hearing the lowly.
The lowly are hearing too.

Letting-free (*Zimzum*) is primal intensity, an extran focus. HE is not in "somethings" but in the letting-free (*Zimzum*). That this is not understood is one of the reasons for the decay of genuine monotheism.

Ritual is directed from and towards the extran focus. Extranity is a new "inner outside" or "outer inside," which is not a new substructure or subconsciousness. A new level!

We are still in a non-world, full of beyondness, images, ontics.

God is a most radical, quasi-bolshevik term.

"The Midst" is attainable.
"Speaking" is immanent.
"The Death-ring" can be broken.

A totally new torsion of the whole is near.

Push back the *Shevirah*—to the passive.
Bring back the *Kizzutz*—to be closed.
Repeat the *Zimzum*—to let free.

The letting-free means the non-possessed world.

The cosmos is flowing into Man.

Without adding a new dimension there is no exit.

Language is the primary wonder.

Ritual is not a "making" but transfunctional.

Among the "objects" of the Ritual are food, breathing, sex. The Ritual changes the functions of Man. The "organic" defies nature.

From heaven to the Midst. Our human constitution is not inherent or natural; it is trialistic, given, commanded.

Three kinds of action: The restful center (Zen), the total devotion (the Bible), the pragmatic efficiency (technology).

We must accept these three: The paradox, the dizziness, the suddenness.

Man is not nature "extended" or "enlarged," but a torsion of the Whole, a turning-point. In turning nature around he also turns himself around.

We do not live in empty "existence," but in that Place (*Makom*) established for us by HIM.

Man is a higher dimension! He can do letting-free (*Zimzum*)—and this is the "highest depth."

The Ritual reaches the focus where the world-lines converge. Therefore it can cause such a profound change, and therefore it is so dynamic.

The cybernetic jumping of the machine over itself is the end of the machine merely as a "robot."

The theophany of the Word. The words on the *prayer-straps* (*Teffilin*) are placed on the head and the arm as *steering orders:* Only the theophany of speech redeems. It lifts up by giving us words that are trialogical and not definitions.

Rising and true speaking are inseparable. The prophet (*Navi*) speaks "upwards."

Ritual words should have a bodily impact and change the body. The ultimate transformation is possible. That we can enter into that sphere is the deepest meaning of the Ritual.

The dichotomic body must be relinquished. The trichotomic body is the ritual body.

Dichotomics are not dialectical but dualistic. Dialectical should mean trichotomous. The step Marx made was dialectical, not "trichotomous."

All dichotomies are exitless. In trichotomies the ways are open.

Body is People, not private. Just this is the mysterium of the body. Man has relapsed into not-being-embraced.

Holiness (*Kadosh*) is an isolated, set-aside region in the Midst of reality, prepared for HIM. There HE can be present.

Three aspects of Ritual: Fullness (*Tahor*), Atonement (*Kippur*), Sanctification (*Kedushah*).

The body has supreme insight, but it has not yet reached "fullness" or "radiance." A new body is needed.

In the religions God has not yet "body."

Everything still is full of images, nothings and destructive forces and therefore unreal.

The "At One," and no spiritual remoteness! The "Near," the "Here," and no postponements!

The Hidden Face (*Anpin Panimayin*)—turned towards us.

We have the capacity of a "doing" that is transfunctional, that knows how to use the "keys." The great discovery: we *can* reach the Midst!

Loosening the biological energies of the people will bring about the highest effects of that "Real Plurality."

The cross-connecting links are missing today. The supernatural physical body is the supernal connecting reality.

A ritualistic total renewal comes out of the depth of the People, not from the individual. It comes from the highest heights, the "dizziness heights."

The physique of the Jews is different. Like all distinctive physiques —if genuinely distinctive—it comes from a Ritual.

Ritual is deepest doing, not a shallow functioning.

The whole cosmos changes, not merely parts of it.

Those who stand in fear and trembling (*Haredim*) are in basic separation from the ontological. There is a "high shaking" in those who are standing upright, a lack of foothold.

Place (*Makom*) overtakes existence. Existence is embedded, has a *Makom*, not vice versa. Whole (*Tam*) is superior to all functions. It is supreme "effect."

From causal mastery to biological mastery is intrinsically ritualistic.

Genuine beginnings happen with suddenness.

Ritual means binding oneself to a steering order.

The deepest home of the Ritual is in the letting-free (*Zimzum*), not in "making." Ritual always "does letting-free (*Zimzum*)."

Jews still have "primal unity."

Rituals, if understood as ontic, are empty and die away.

Ritual is directed against Platonism.

Totems—the primal ram, the golden calf, the red cow—are relapses, not merely pre-stages.

"Man is the Messiah of nature." (Novalis)

God has a worldly destiny.

The big step now is to discard the dichotomic body, which is only an anti-mind body. Unity-body in place of anti-mind body.

Accept the fact that body has highest information. Body is the greatest "object" of all Ritual. Only now Ritual again reaches the body. *We must reach the pre-biological not only the inorganic.*

Jewishness is an undiluted "Here." No "Beyond."

Consummation is not the "end" but the "beginning." The maximal body is possible.

The real plurality puts an end to the body-soul riddle.

In mathematics mind and body meet.

The ingathering of the unconscious is one of the highest possibilities of Man.

The finite can be pure through Ritual! To deny this is the great mistake of spiritualistic "religiosity."

No envelope can ever become an "object," because one enters into the envelope and is not "faced" with it.

Can technology become theophanic? Yes! Cybernetically. By the redemption of the machine, the robot!

Body and face are formed by the Ritual. Body has highest purity, far superior to merely ideological purity.

Nothing else but the Ritual can overtake the raging techniques.

Images—the arts—are still magical.

Capitalism is without speech; it defines, gives labels for merchandise (Kafka's "Oddradek").

Why do the nations rage? There is a threefold raging. The three ontics are raging. Why? Because they are not genuine, and what is weak, rages.

God is not dead but uninvolved, and because of that an ultra-radical revolution is needed.

Between God and Man is only the Word and no intermediaries. *The Word is spoken*. This is a most profound insight.

God and body must meet in the *Shiur Komah*, and not, as now, body and death. The ritualistic body is the deathless body. It does not die, it is death-free.

Without Man there would be no worlds. Man "envelops" nature.

Reality comes in "quants" or discontinuities. Without Man there would be no worlds. Man "envelops" nature.

Ritual is an attitude that presupposes only The One.

"Only the Lowly understand the Torah!"

Exodic—Exilic—Extranic.

The Absolute Call: "Where art thou" (*efo hayekha*) was heard only once.

A new bursting-open of the primal layer is imminent, a radical doing-away with all magic. Only then does HE emerge, over and beyond all images.

No ultimate "layers" or "stuff," but Ritual. "The Primal Scale" is suspended from the "Nothing."

The third (cybernetics) is neither subject nor object nor spirit nor matter. It is trans-dichotomic.

"In itself" suspends itself since Kant. Loneliness is the amorality of the "in-itself." A dichotomic world cannot stand. The "thing-in-itself" is dissolved in ethics, for the world is an ethical not an ontic phenomenon. Now we must complete Kant!

The cosmological maximum is the sociological minimum.

Reality is "created" not primal.

Extran thinking is not attached to any subject. It is detached.

This is potentially the deepest aspect of communism if it were a ritual behavior.

The plurality-body is not merely a concept. Body is never without People. Otherwise it would be dichotomic, a spook, not a genuine body. It would be private, when it should be public.

Speech rises above definitions toward the meta-language. Definitions are not "words." Not meta-physics, but meta-language. Theophany is now in Speech!

Because we have no presence there can be no presence with us. God is absent because *we* are absent. HE is not in any "something-reality," nor in anything which "grasps itself." If *we* would "do letting-free (*Zimzum*)," HE would emerge.

The primal break: Grasping was chosen before *Life*. This was the *Kizzutz*, the separation of the Two Trees in the Garden of Eden.

Two ways we can go—to the mechanical (owning) or to the ritualistic (binding, embracement).

No Platonic-Christian contempt for the body. The body can be pure and sacred.

One cannot pierce-through the "in-itself," but one can pierce-through the "ring of death," the images, powers and things. Extranity is attainable, purity is attainable.

Without corporeality HE is lost. HIS Body is the new corporeality. The *Threeness-Experience* is an immediate experience. We are Three, God—Man—World, irreducibly and inseparably in this order.

Murder is a doing out of emptiness, out of irreality. It is fury without strength; the greater the emptiness the greater the fury.

Fullness of reality is not compatible with doing or functioning; it is ritualistic.

De-do, dis-do and un-do the doing!

Matter is not understandable as matter but, in the last analysis, as the Body of God (*Shiur Komah*).

God is not in the theologies, HE is in the Rituals.

The set-free language means the end of all "terms," particularly the metaphysical, religious ones. They are empty and hollowed out.

The *Zimzum* is not a technique but Ritual. The *Kizzutz* is not a technique but cybernetical. Technique can be turned upside down. Turn it upside down!

The Melting Point: Do not ask, how can this melting, this summation be brought about, but do ask, what has brought about this non-summation, this non-melting?

The enormous truth needed today is not encompassed in the individual, but rather in the *real plurality*, which we can enter. (This accessibility is the *Great Now*.) Ritually—not functionally—we can become part of it.

The schizophrenia of our doing is challenged by the Ritual.

Ritual is implicit in the *Dwelling of the People*. It is call, nearness, commission, command. It is without any loneliness.

From doing to hearing (*Nasse ve nishma*) is an ascending.

The way by which the body will be transformed is not natural but ritualistic. Nature is exhausted; the Ritual can re-emerge. In the Ritual there is nothing cognitive, no remoteness, no later, only the here-and-now, with no margin for mistakes. Ritual mistakes are inherently deadly.

Real speaking is a "standing upright." He who is standing upright must speak or he will die.

"En-man" the split and "de-man" the substructures.

"Normalcy" is useless. No appeal to nature or convention! Just "miracles" will do!

There is no "nature"; nature is history.

"Above and beyond" is no *heaven;* there is only Man rising ever higher.

"Down and below" is the *lowly depth,* the *depth of the People* (*Itarutah*).

The Midst is more than a location. It is place (*Makom*). It is inhabited. It speaks. The critical Essenic mistake is that the People are lost, the Below rejected, Man given up. The teachings of Paul invalidated the Ritual, and by pseudo-Messianism cut short history, which opposes all eschatologies, short-cuts, escapings, evadings.

"Outside" is neither inessential nor empty, but extran. There the individual is radiant, let-free and becomes ritualistic. Reality is "Adamic" or not understandable at all.

Our ability for Ritual is obscured by pragma. Ritual presupposes a theophoric People. There is none today.

God's absence is now the primal, basic factuality, not that HE does not "exist."

Resurrection of the dead (*tediyath ha metim*) implies that the Ritual-body can be regained even after death. Says Job: "From within my flesh I shall see HIM"—not in a Beyond.

Ritual is trans-practical. The pragma (the functional) is waste-stuff out of the *Kizzutz,* the primal schizophrenia. To restore the Ritual, restore the unbrokenness of action.

To "lay Teffilin" means the head, the heart and the hand tied, focused by the Name (*Shem*), three simultaneities, shaping a new body.

Holiness is not in a Beyond. It is Holiness of the World.

Genuine Peoplehood is enveloped ritualistically.

Only Man is an "image" (made in HIS Image).

Ritual-doing can out-do pragma-doing. It can be total change, mutation.

We experience now an extreme "telescoping" of everything into one point, a turning-point from which new dimensions can be reached.

The robot is externalizable in cybernetics. Cybernetics means jumping over oneself and over one's own shadow. It also means, more is coming out than has been put in.

We already are outside of nature, moving beyond the things, the powers and the pictures.

God's Presence is in *Zimzum*. "Somethings" are in *Kizzutz*.

The primeval sources of our body are not in the natural, but in the Ritual. A heap of bricks is not a house; the house transcends the bricks. Nature-body is merely such raw-material. The Ritual-body is genuinely Man-like.

Body is not the most "private"; it is a supreme openness. The People is in each body.

The new body-theology has nothing in common with those religions which are merely spiritual and not ritualistic.

The alternative to declining religions is not materialism, but the Presence of the Name and body-theology.

The Ritual, a unity of primeval origins, makes possible an almost unlimited rising higher. Real plurality, united ritually, can achieve almost anything.

The institutionalized religions are obsolete, the *Presence of the Name* is not.

Extranity, the Midst and the Name do not imply a "heaven," but a radicalized "earth."

Jonah cried out from inside the monster. We are settling-down in its belly!

Monotheism without its numinosity loses its strength.

Spinoza's three errors: (1) God is "cause" (*causa sui*). (2) God or nature (*deus sive natura*). (3) God unrelated to Man. That HE addresses Man viewed as superstition.

The animal has come to an end; what is still left is merely dross. It was "totem," it is not so now.

The multiplicity-reality is not a metaphorical conception; it is primal. To establish it as a reality can only be done ritualistically.

The Ritual does not emerge from the individual, but from the real plurality. It is reflected in the individual as a member of that plurality.

"People" is possible only ritualistically, not politically or organizationally. The People's summit, the People's depth, the People's midst are ritualistic.

Nature cannot answer the human question. Nature came to an end, animal came to an end. What is imminent now? *Man* has come into his own. Everything has been delegated to Man!

Genuine thinking speaks. It must not be silent; speechless thinking cannot be called thinking. The new theophany is in speech, in the word.

The conventional misconception of the Bible is that the Old Testament is a mere pre-stage to the higher development reached by the New Testament. There is no such! There is not a rising but a declining from the primal radicalism and concreteness.

The humanity of the *Great Flood* (*Mabul humanity*), violence-ridden and power-ridden was united but demonic. If united in a holy way it could not have been annihilated.

Four Issues of the End of History:
(1) Cybernetics. Not an evading, but another depth-dimension.

The new vision of what is a "machine" is a transition from the era of technology to the era of cybernetics.

(2) The new theology, which is not "Heaven-Theology" but "Midst-Theology." The Bible is regained.

(3) The end of nature. Nature is "circum-hominized."

(4) Deep down in the body is the new abode (*Makom*), a new corporeality. The connection of what is Divine with the body means no dichotomy any longer!

TABLE OF THE BROTHERHOOD OF MAN

Hosea—the humble bearer of our burden. "Enveloped envelopment." The three primal moments (*Zimzum—Shevirah—Kizzutz*) are embraced by Man.

The new Zimzum is delegated by God to Man. Man answers. He responds to the *Zimzum*, withdrawing from the three "nothings" or three "itnesses" (images, powers, things), and goes back to his own "essence," his own "destiny." Man is unfettered. Every form of owning, power and privilege is the strongest and most effective form of ontic perversion. Therefore a genuine revolution, in its profoundest sense, would be a ritual pattern.

The new Shevirah is the relativization of nature and the consignment of nature to Man. The original Creation sank down into *nature,* usurping absoluteness, but has now been relegated to passivity by mathematics. It is a "Farewell to mother nature." Science starts with the birth of Man.

The new Kizzutz. The primal split is quite manifest now, and the return to the Ritual is the only alternative. The split cannot be closed by passively staring into it, but by embracing it with the full stature of Man. This will heal the breach of substructure and superstructure.

The result: We will be released for our higher destiny. On the old level there are no exits, no answers, no higher spheres.

"Thinking is mightier than being!"

THE NEW ZIMZUM

Ritual is the main issue! Ritual vs. pragma.

Discard the dichotomic body and do not settle down inside of the "monster."

The *Shiur Komah-body* is not dichotomic.

The limit of nature has come with relativity. It can no longer ascend because Man is surrounding it!

Pre-biology and Ritual rise to higher levels, to a *primal plurality*, which is not a "resultant" or additive.

The Body of God (*Shiur Komah*) is not ontic; it gives names, speaks, but is not an "is."

Nothing ontic is Divine. Only HE, Who created out of nothing.

Everything should be expressed in terms of the Midst, not of ontics.

Man outside of himself. The body of Man is not "nature" but Ritual.

The "postponement" has run its course. There is only the "Now."

The "numinous fear" is primal. The death-fear is not.

The Ritual-sphere, all encompassing, is the deepest stratum.

My body is HIS Body. Body-theology is the profoundly new attitude. The "new body" brings a total change. The inhabited Midst replaces all theologies.

All "somethings" are holes. Reality has a letting-free *Zimzum*-like quality.

Death is impurity (*Tumah*), a Ritual-failure.

Finiteness is not the issue.

The plurality-body is not the private individual body. It is the God body, the Ritual-body. This new body is not matter, not an "anti," but *Shiur*.

It will be a majestic revelation when we understand the language of the body.

Influence of Yoga on the body: downwards, dissolving!
Influence of Ritual on the body: upwards, ascending!

Yoga liberates from the body. Ritual elevates and enhances the body. Ritual is "polar" in contrast to Yoga.

Christianity has lost its front-position. It is losing its relevance to the advanced facts in science, revolution, Ritual.

Death is not a negation, not a breaking-up, but an opening-up of a new dimension. Death can be removed. It is not a physico-natural, but one of corruption or impurity. This is the point at issue, not finiteness. Finiteness is not the same as death. Finiteness, if ritualistically pure, is indestructible!

Aphorisms and Affirmations

Truth from which emerges—people. People from which emerges—truth.

Things are intrinsically merchandise, not only "can become" so. Ontology is a form of indifferentism. So is logical positivism. But the question is whether there is such an indifferent *reality*. Socio-analysis may demask logical positivism. All ontology is sociological escape.

The openness of Man. Man *is* seen. The split man is closed; the closed man is split. The transcendence of man is his most genuine, distinguishing quality; logic and ethics are the manifestations of it. Philosophy, as extremism, demands the Whole of Man. No basic change without healing the basic split. Unification never is merely technical or organizational, but ultimately ethical.

The entropy of philosophy. All great human movements fizzle out or are running into vicious circles. The radical directness of the world can only be shown, and this is the profundity of a mystical pragmatism.

Reality is an ethical not an ontological conception. It is related even to sex-behavior.

The *whole* is not the maximal—it is only the whole of the *given*. Above and beyond the whole is the *meaning*. A whole can be meaningless, because it can be without inner freedom. A whole can—or must—swing outside of its own nature. This swinging-out is its true life.

Selves are not things. This is a universe that contains Man.

The great fallacy of attempts to coordinate views is that they level all events and aspects onto one plane, the lowest possible plane. (A well-known exemplification is to see the Bible as "tribal legends," which is to measure it with the lowest yardstick. What is not seen is the autonomous, vertical structure of the text.)

The phenomena show their real life when they are free of all ontological qualities. But ours is a demonic world! (Not that without God certain problems cannot be solved, but that without God the deepest and greatest problems would not even emerge.)

A phenomenology of action is needed. Action is not an organizing or managing, it is spontaneous, free. There is a suddenness and an autonomy of true action. It must be understood in its own terms. Abraham's *"Here I am"* (*Hineni*) is a readiness without any transition or way or "how to," but an immediate answer to a call without a fraction of time in-between.

Ontology asks "what is"—ethics what "should be." The messianic view asks what "will be."

Judaism is not a power-system, and this is the reason for its sanity.

The Absolute is facing Man—not Man the Absolute. Prayers are revolutionary outcries. Not "to read" the Bible, but to *call it out*. The true word *addresses*, not only *says* something. The true body has its roots in the word, not in nature. The true word can purify the body, making the body transparent.

All causality is magic because it gives power to things, making the world demonic. The purified world is power-free. Magic is a form of violence. Violence is magic. The causal reality is demonic. Whitehead's God as the "principle of concretion" is HE Who Sets Limits (the *El Shadai*).

Things are unethical. The deepest root of what we call matter is in ethics not in science. Scientific materialism is outdated, for sociology is replacing ontology. For us, God is not really God—man not man—world not world.

The phenomena around us are neither real nor unreal, but *not-yet* real. Reality must be free from impurity, must be accepted, confronted and must answer. The phenomena do not "answer" yet, because we have not entered the world yet. Decision is not possible on objective grounds. This would not be freedom. The mere "choice between" is either arbitrary, or—if not made—neurosis ensues.

The question is not only equal rights but *right* rights. The ruling classes always have been more class-conscious than the proletariat.

One of the schools of Existentialism, the atheistic school, is a kind of naturalism, even if it uses human terms, because these terms are deprived of their human meaning.

From the basic paradox to the basic split. The Antinomies (Kant) mirror the basic split. The paradox is Divine, the split is sickness, yet superior to what is called "normalcy."

The socio-psycho-ethico analysis of the "thing." Why is it fallen into thinghood?

Transcending is analogous to revolution, ontology analogous to property. The transcending individuals are alive and able to meet; the closed ones clash. To restore the world would be a profound revolution, a transformation beyond imagination. If things and thoughts were not only amalgamated but integrated, then a higher dimension would be reached and both would show new qualities.

Heisenberg: "Position" is blurred the more we go back—or ahead. Through long distances also all identity disappears ever more. An apparent "clear" identity is only a transition for a short moment. (A number is such a transitory point of the relatively "greatest" condensation of a process.) The Biblical YES vs. NO. God embraces but does not obliterate. Anxiety in its deepest is confrontation with nothingness, with perdition.

HE surrounds all worlds (*sovev kol almim*). (Compare Whitehead's idea of the "envelopes.") God is not cause but "dwelling." But how to change the world so that HE can be present? The emergent plane is "theophanic." Always? Now? The place of God is being taken by something that "exists," that is "owned." God is not "ownable." The Divine Call is for Change.

The principle of ontology is idolatrous.
The principle of psychology is perverted.
The principle of sociology is murderous.

The "Whole" can easily be idolatrized. The "Whole" is only one more quality. Demasking ontology as property-aspect, as owning, as haptic-bias, as nutrition-anxiety. *There are no indifferent realities.*

The greater the goal the greater the freedom. Mere absence of all resistance is not freedom but chaos.

Only Non-Power-Collectives can persist. All Power-Collectives must go insane. God is not power but truth. There may be a pragmatic force to falsehood, the useful lie.

God is the God of the future. Abraham was overwhelmed by the fear of the Absence of God. The invisible can be perceived with the heart. Faith is not a theoretical, but a practical behavior.

Mere "existence" is a meaningless term, even self-contradictory.

In nature all beings are derived from one another. But in history there are spontaneous, genuine novelties. Yet—there is a historical element also in nature. And this higher dimension which envelops nature is what makes for the ascending trend of nature.

The togetherness that aims at calling the exiled God back to earth is Israelic togetherness.

There is no other freedom than "on the Tablets." Freedom has no other meaning than being capable of positive action. "The reward of good action is that action itself," an autonomous attitude.

Truth is theocratic and practical in one. Infinite possibilities are tantamount to chaos.

A genuine People can never be constituted by power. Only nations can; they are power-groups. If a nation sets-up itself as superior, or claims global superiority, the moment has come to get rid of all Israelic structures. This is a historical rule. It also applies to the present powers.

That Man *is* seen is one of the profoundest aspects of faith in God. Seeing, then, has a polar even dialectical character. The radical mistake is to surrender man to the production-process. This is the actual form of the basic schizophrenia of man today. Man is sinking back into thinghood—into "dust."

When the basic functions of man are not reached and involved, change cannot occur. Functions concerned with the sustenance and propagations of life are still "substructure," and the higher functions "superstructure." The substructure becomes demonical, the superstructure ideological. Both are unreal and mutually destructive.

The Arts: A form of pre-action (pre-existence), magic action, not redeemed action. Art is a form of mercifulness, a non-deserved consolation, a not-achieved harmony, a non-concrete beauty.

There are no general patterns of life, but messages (propositions) to concrete situations. Everyone is a First Man, not only derived, but also new.

The Divine Withdrawal	*Demonization of Nature*	*The Split of Man*
The Transcendence of God	The Breaking of the Vessels	The Adamic Collapse

The single and the general are still separated, because the single do not form a community. The community does not allow singles.

What is the mission, specifically, of this specific moment? Breaking through what we call the causality-structure!

The *depth* of life surpasses the *length* of life.

Impurity is not a "lack" but a very tangible quality (*tumah*).

The determinism of history is negative: the imperfect, the corrupted, the split cannot persist. This is the only limitation which is determined.

The paradox of goal and freedom. Does the goal not exclude freedom? This is a *profound* paradox. Highest freedom is to materialize goals, it is not the absence of all givenness. Givenness and freedom are not contradictory. Yet: the *something* from which the pagan starts is problematic. Starting from the *nothing* of creation arrives at something.

The *H C* !
THE HUMAN CONTINUUM
is the maximal Continuum

A *Corpus Mysticum*—the Human Continuum (*H C*) is not a natural but a Man-made community; not by "identity" (animistic), but by "participation."

Action can be merely practical, or it can be eternity in action, Absolute Presence. Action, not merely technical, historical, religious, personal or collective, but overwhelmingly immediate and valid.

Beyond the polarities such as: unchangeable, evolutionary, mind—matter, or space—time, lie integrations which reveal a higher realm. But after the class-division a new split may emerge, touching the deepest ground, beyond the exhaustion of all given planes.

The difference between seeing and hearing is basic, much more than the mere difference between two senses. Hearing transcends and leans over the edge of the world. Seeing sees into the world.

The basic schizophrenia: *Why the split between the given and the ideal?*

The problem of eschatology is already in the question: Why do we see the objects "outside there"? The components of this epistemological relation are looked at as "indifferent substances." But such "indifferents" cannot communicate. The conception of "apprehension" being dualistic is fallacious from the very start. "Two" cannot be connected. The act of *perception* is a transcending of the subject, not a "grasping," "getting"; it is an act of swinging outwards, not a privacy. Epistemology is pre-Marxist. Man is basically open. Therefore the epistemological position is intrinsically fallacious. A fictitious question! Perception is not "passive" but a real going outside. Man is closed only in so far as he is split. The closed, private person is the bourgeois, regardless of his status otherwise.

Yet, there is a legitimate dualism; a dialectical, ethical, revolutionary dualism of perpetually being thrown against the Absolute. There is indeed a *"Geworfensein"* (Heidegger), not against nothingness but against reality! "Nothingness" understood as the "nothingness" of the *Divine Creation out of nothing* and hence antagonistic to the abyss.

An infinitely deeper penetration of the world is needed. The world is the object of science—but the world is creation.

A phenomenology of death—death as such—not the belittled death that belongs to the spook-immortality. A profounder conception of death is a pre-condition of the deeper penetration of life.

The mystery of integration into higher relations of all phenomena puts the stream of life in the light of a higher rotation. (Maximalized, accepted, purified, integrated.)

The "symbolized" Bible is utterly a-religious. God as "existent" or coordinated with—whatever it may be—is atheism. God can be realized by man only in empirical transcendence, that makes for a bursting of all existence.

The image is lost to imagination because tied to pictorial thinking, which ruins both mind and imagination.

Immortality is not a post-mortem affair; it is an autonomy of levels, of resistance against disintegration inside of life. It is a faculty of life, beyond the immortality of the individual person.

Rebellion is not neurotic; but the stopped or frustrated revolt entails a neurosis.

Two fears: The nothingness-fear and the abundance-fear. "Anxiety" is not concerned with concrete single issues or facts. It is general— it is our anxiety about existence.

The world has an origin and a goal and is suspended between the two. Each moment in its process represents the whole of it in ever new forms, totality and singularity united.

Religion should be: the *relation* between God—Man—World; it should not be concerned with the "essence" of God. Man and the World are no less mysterious than God. A profound saying: "One must never utter the NAME without Man and the World."

Earnestness—Unification—Purity—are the condition for attaining concreteness. Israel as a pariah-revolt is basically not-normal. The Bible speaks of the social exile as the genuine drama of humanity, and not of metaphysical events in the realm of archetypes or substances.

What is the Universal Name of all things? In what "class" is that?

The two polar tendencies: transcending and immanence—to be radicalized; only then can they be integrated. Radical transcending —radical worldliness! It is the world that makes higher and higher mundane experience emerge.

The objections against the idea of God refer to the theologized, idolatrized God. The idolatrization of God is a fundamental fallacy, closing the *open* world. The attachment of God to each and every single is most Divine. God is the "Absolutely," not the lonely. God "alone" becomes "thing." (Compare: an electron alone ceases to exist.) God as "epi-phenomenon" is no God.

The biological field surrounds the physical field. It has a higher integration. The physical field is not ultimate reality. Biology has its own logic, its own time. Physics is only a useful abstraction from this higher field. Physics has to be seen in the light of higher structures. Vitalism tried to add one more force—the vital-force, a fallacious view which, moreover, does not succeed in rising to a higher level than physics. Yet even biological reality is not ultimate reality.

Man—*at the Tree* neutralizes the thesis of the universe, because he breaks down the fundamental demarcation-line between *knowing* and *life* to an indifferent "existing." In choosing the "tree of knowledge of good and evil" he forgets that this difference is not a mere object of knowledge but an object of *decision*.

Reality and unreality are mixed in the phenomena. The fate of the cosmos hinges on the actual issues. There is a moment—time and again—when the cosmos is actualized.

The Kabbalah undertook to speak about our fears and hopes, about nature and about things in terms of monotheistic holiness. Man alone with nature would be speechless. No speech is possible with nature, nor with archetypes and substructures. They cannot be "addressed!" Speech pre-supposes a reality which is addressable. The highest degree of humanness was reached by Man when Moses was addressed by God "as one man speaks to his neighbor."

There are *em*ergents and *sub*mergents.

All religions are retrogressive or remnants of primordial situations, of other-worldliness. Yet there is a tremendous force in the religions that can be reversed, and then they could serve the people. But only the radical Biblical religion can undergo such change without losing its identity. We will have to wrest religion from the hands of reactionary powers to establish openness. Holiness transcends. Logic transcends. Ethics transcends.

The Redemption of Action! What matters is: What is the goal of action—what is the object of action?
The goal: Power. This means bridging insufficiencies, perversions, failures. Action remains power-action, insane.
The object: Today a fictitious reality. No free spontaneous action possible on fictitious objects. Such action on irreality is, and can only be, violence. All actions on irrealities are magical and fictitious!
Result: Action still is magic. Redeemed action is ethical and not magical. China's "Wu Wei" knew full well the problem of the demonic character of what is called action and the difference between action of the broken violent soul and the integrated peaceful soul.

Empirical paradoxes are possible. (Michelson's experiment.) Accepting the paradox was Einstein's first and decisive step. Then everything else followed as a consequence of this step.

Does the Whole move to a higher level? The fundament would change then, although the distance between "bottom" and "Man" may be relatively the same. But the whole process would occur on a higher level. This motion would be perceived as an analogous— physical motion. Body, so far as it is understood as matter, is a mathematical structure. "De-onionize" the fictitious world!

Are all the electrons or atoms (of one type) equal? If there are no two equal things—which is doubtless true—what then about "equal" electrons (or atoms, or molecules)? The equals are identicals! The differences are in positions, not in structures. Therefore an entirely new aspect of "electronic multitudes" is needed. There are only a rather limited number of physical situations, and the "particles" are pictorial descriptions of that order. Therefore the "omni-presence" of a particle or the "mixed-up-ness" (Whitehead) of all things. There is the reality of the identity of "particles" and the "extrinsic" reality of the differences of their positions.

Moses' "Hear oh Heaven" is a mighty gesture, silencing the cosmos and demanding that it should listen to his proclamation of the NAME, establishing sovereignty of the NAME over nature.

Naturalism does not do justice to nature, because it is merely a frustration-failure conception, projected outside. The world without exit (not transcending) cannot be established. No polarity produces a current without actualization of both poles. There are no "hen-egg-problems," or "first cause problems." "Hen-egg" are one.

Place (*Makom*) is a truly great Name of God; it has also a profound relation to the world, which has a place. The world that *has* a place and the world that has *none* are in deepest antagonism.

Since Man factually *is* in the cosmos, then this is a cosmos built so that it produces Man and may have Man as its goal. Concepts such as "substance," "matter," "object," "subject," "spirit" are completely empty. *Wanted*: Concepts of intensity of participation.

That the world has been "created" is a most revolutionary vision, because it establishes a purposeful reality of change and process. It superimposes history on the universe, makes the universe "historical."

Moulding a people's body into a focused, transparent body that is autonomous towards the disintegration of the bodily structure too, detaches it from the psychological substructure (incest, perversions, fixations). Verticalism! This does not mean "one line" (linear) but a manyfold, higher dimensionality, cumulative, transcending.

What step could be more consequential than the unification of Man beyond his brokenness, preparing him for a life of plenty—so far utterly unmastered.

Salvation of the Arts. Only one way: beauty attached, not "beauty as such!" Subordination of the Arts under the human purposes.

God as present and as absent (Kafka: A Divine World abandoned by God.) Profane is in Hebrew *Chul* (sand), pulverized and without focus, the people dissolved into "singles." The art of living without reality is the up-to-date style.

World is the sphere of maximal realization of tension. The movement of the lower moves the higher.

Righteousness (*Zedakah*) is "active truth," not only "justice." The irrational cannot simply be opposed; it has to be included in the realm of the mind and to be harnessed. The therapy—to live up to a more perfect type of Man.

The neighbor—that is he with whom we have the most direct, nearest contact. To love all is to love nobody. To love "love" is not love.

Property should not only be taken away from the hands, but from the heads and the hearts.

God not to be reached by a devaluation of the world but by a *fulfillment* of the world. By devotion! Even by revolutionary demands. Maximalism—Verticalism—Holism.

A most decisive step: explaining not in terms of ontology but in terms of action. The images are tools not entities. To pervert this rule is the sin of the Arts. The subordination of the images is akin to the subordination of nature, that is to Man. A relation: the expanding universe and the "breaking of the vessels" (*shevirah ha kelim*).

The world is concrete, not made of "generalities." The concrete event manifests the prototype, which has "to be done." The concrete can do what no prototype can do. The *basic person* must be reached and influenced. The essential Marxian method is: to become conscious of one's own class and condition. But this has not happened yet. There is hardly a mobilization of man's highest, deepest, strongest incentives. The ultimate radicalism is the final unity (*Yihud*).

No power-conception has any objective scientific value. All such conceptions are capitalistic projections onto science.

There is no "uni"-verse. Property and anxiety are bound up together. Reality, on the other hand, is communicability. Real change will not come from politics but from philosophy.

Whatever is detached from man becomes destructive, so the production-process.

God against nothingness *and* against the "beyond." Lay claim to the "Here!" The world is established *against nothingness*; the full world, pure, united, stands against perdition.

The less concerned with God but with the world as God's world, the clearer will HE emerge.

Universalism is possible only on a very high level, otherwise it is conformism.

Haldane's "intrinsic organization." The living organism is not a secondary, derived quality but omnipresent. Not "somewhere" but "everywhere," even on the molecular or sub-molecular level. Newtonian physics and chemistry collapse when applied to the living organism. "Organism" is the basic principle (Whitehead). Life has the same right to be regarded as essential as the Galilean principles!

Impurity (*Tumah*) is a positive quality not only an absence of purity.

All pre-human mentality is now obsolete, even discarded.

| Creation | Revelation | Redemption |
| Relativity | Verticality | Unity |

Is the substructure or the abyss basic? Abyss!

Emergent evolution is an Exodus of Man. Man is the Exodus-principle. Evolution is not linear (in the old sense) but has several dimensions. The basic line from which the variety of species emerges is moving. The whole of the living realm ascends. If the novelties were merely to come from the Whole, the Total, would not make them novelties. The genuine novelties presuppose a motion of the Whole!

The problem of "the Goose in the Bottle" (Zen Buddhism)—how to get it out without breaking the bottle—is the problem of Man in the world, how to free him without breaking the world by asceticism, mortification or killing. The answer in Zen: "OUT" is no answer in the Western technical sense. Yet, the profundity of that "OUT" is that it is above the ordinary procedures, ways, methods and managing. The "OUT" is a higher dimension. (Such as shows up also in n-dimensional modern mechanics.) The most important analogy is the Biblical. "Here I am" (*Hineni*), the immediacy of action, with nothing "in between." This immediacy and directness is beyond all thingness. The "meaning of suddenness." The present crisis of humanity is no longer susceptible of gradual cures. The "OUT" is primal. (Man surrounds the "bottle of nature.")

Connection is solely a human category, there are no other connections or fusions. Nothing "influences" anything. All other connections demand "identity." All identity is reductive. Identity as a levelling principle also is akin to thingness and belongs deeply to mass-production! Leibniz and the end of "identity." There are no two equal things. So connection is human, social; any other connection is destructive.

Matter and Spirit cannot be united. *The Face and the Word can! This* is the integration we are looking for! Only on *that* level can it be found.

Our "body" is not "matter"; our "mind" is not "spirit." Body is not —intrinsically—destined for putrefaction. Mind is not—intrinsically —an empty "abstraction." Mind is the only legitimate, not-demonic force.

The Creation has to be derived from the Creator, not vice versa. The enigma is Man.

Accept God and the World becomes a paradox, an object for revolution.

Man dropped, given up, the prerequisite for mass-production.

"AND," a basic word. The first "AND" in Heaven *and* Earth.

ACTION   ETHICS   LOGIC

Action is not merely "doing," "making," "organizing," "effort." Not gradual, but sudden. It is *Absolute Freedom, Absolute Spontaneity*, the moment when the Vertical cuts into the Horizontal.

Ethics is not merely "habits," "customs," "morals." It is the *Absolute Requirement*, the *Divine Confrontation*, not present until God is accepted by Man. The Ethical Task can *not* emerge without God.

Logic is not merely "calculating," "concluding," "analyzing," it is "finding," "exploring," "speaking," "ascending"; it is synthetic.

The perfect integration of God's remoteness and nearness. The immediate relation of God to each, to each man, to each event and each moment is not through the medium of general ideas or any intermediaries. The fallacy of understanding God as a "general idea," guiding the world indirectly by a certain order. HIS directness to "eachness," the Holiness of absolute transcendence and remoteness gives us the guarantee for infinite enhancement.

The theophanic character of the present conflict of mankind repeats —in modern terms—the *Kizzutz*.

The object as "the thing in itself" came to an end, and the unified, not-split object emerges as a Divine Unity. There is none other. No other "One" but the Divine ONE!

On the Possibility of
Regaining a Ritual Existence

This is the deepest, the central, the towering problem of our time. It makes most other problems and possibilities shrink to almost a trifle. Such a shrinking of circumstances and conditions is a signal for a new beginning, which always starts exactly at such a point. It is on this pivot that we must focus, where now all previous history seems to merge, and the unfolding of new horizons begins. (Compare: The theory of the cosmic beginning from one "point.")

"Doing"—*all* doing now falls under a question-mark. It is utterly sick. This is the root of the nihilistic tendencies of today. There is a Point (*Nekudah*), an innermost focus for our "doing," anterior to thought, ideas and theories. (Although we must not forget that there is also a kind of "changing of places," since theory too can precede all practice as positional.) This by no means refers to the *fictional* difference between theory and practice, but rather to the difference or antithesis between ethics and magic, the pure and the impure, life and death. The deep-rooted *primal point* of "doing" is first and last anti-magical! All "doings" culminating in *results* are technical, pragmatic and idealistic (Platonic). They are magical vicious circles, self-annihilating because there is no way from "results" to "action."

The mighty "we will do and hear" (*naaseh ve nishmah*) of the Torah and the "Jewish way," has this ever been fully understood? It would be superficial to interpret it simply as the "primacy" of doing.

It rather means that in the deepest sense "doing and hearing" are one. Here we are at the threshold of the crucial question of mankind's apocalyptic situation today: the "ritual-catalepsy," apparent in the total inability of modern man to live by a ritual.

This "we will do and hear" has been interpreted by Orthodoxy in too commonplace a way, coordinating "doing" with everyday "doing," which indeed has fallen sick. "Doing" *and* "ritualistic doing" then decay, together with the perverted actions of a dying social order. The hierarchy of action and the real meaning of the distinction between clean and unclean doing are not considered. This levelling-down is the enemy of genuine Orthodoxy. Orthodoxy is vulnerable today not because it is too radical but because it is not radical enough. It is not ready for the Biblical Revolution. It proclaims the "still great" instead of the "still-to-be-great."

The two poles of our existence, the profoundest depth and the sublimest height, are so far only vaguely connected because we do not see the swinging-out of the self over itself, nor the penetrating into the "higher spheres" (*Hekhaloth*), encompassing and embracing the lower ones. In these envelopes new "emergents" arise, not merely "resultants." Outdated verbiage obscures and blurs the "word" and its correspondent, the "definition." Pragmatic and magical "doing" are demonic and lethal.

The radical here-and-now of Jewish action is not negated by acknowledging the deadly crisis of pragmatic action. What should be rejected is the thaumaturgy, which has befallen the Biblical demand of pure action. Orthodoxy cannot forestall the danger of a complete decay of the Ritual, or the hostility against the Ritual brought about by equating the sick paralyzed action within a rotten social order with the genuine pure action of the Ritual. The crisis lies in the "doing," not in the Ritual.

There is a twofold non-problematic view of the Ritual. *Orthodoxy*: there is no problem involved, just do it!
Secularism: it is not important, for what matters is the ethical life. The Ritual is not directly concerned with ethical improvements; it aims at the ever-renewed fundaments of a people and at the sources of ethical possibilities, which should include the body. "Rite" properly means "the way one goes," exactly the same as the Hebrew

term *halakhah*. It means an extraneous knowing and doing, not subjective, not solipsistic, but transpersonal and transpragmatic.

The "nisus" of the cosmos (the rising higher of the universe) is the fundamental event in nature. But this onrush has come to an end in Man. Is Man the end? A blind alley? The anguish of Nietzsche and the doubts of Freud raise the question whether Man is a blunder of nature.

This is the all-surpassing event, above and beyond the historical "point" of today: *the nisus is delegated to Man*. Not God became Man, but nisus became Man! Will Man accept this or will he sink back? Will the nisus of the billions of years come to a stop with us? Arrived at the "point" (the condensation of all previous events), this momentous hour demands: A *new* and still more radical *exile* and a new return (*teshuvah*).

The crisis of the Ritual is rooted in the apocalypse of "doing." Is Man possible? Is Man finally on his own or lost? Is this a transition-stage only? Will it be possible for us to enter into a new sphere of higher "binding"? All previous *"devotions"* are outlived and empty: the cultural, religious, political as well as the philosophical, social and economic are gone or almost gone. None has anything to offer except the Ritual. There is, however, one important presupposition—namely that the Ritual must be separated from "practicalism." "Practical" today becomes "non-practical" in a continuous process of self-destruction. *The practical by itself is demonic.* The Ritual is not part of practical action, not an effect; it establishes reality, endows us with reality, which can be bestowed on us but can also be taken away. Out of this reality flows "pure action." Purity (*tahor*) is not an evading, not emptiness, not a "keeping aloof from something," not an attempt to avoid incurring guilt, not Christian or Buddhistic, but a maximal change, a revolutionary transformation into genuine life.

Israel's segregation (*segolah*) is not a going away from one's fellow-man, but a going up to Zion (*aliyah*). Purity detaches itself from impurity (*tumah*), from corruption and death, but not from Man. This was the mistake of the Essenes. The Pharisees (the segregated) did not make this mistake, but remained *inside* of the People. And because of that they never lost—as the Essenes did—the Ritual.

These loving segregationists did not end up in Paulinism or Christianity.

The Ritual now must liberate the lost domain of action from its entanglement with perversion. This disentangling will be one of the most difficult efforts ever made to save Man from extinction. Will we end in a zero-point or will we conquer it to pass through it? It could very well be that mankind has to take this supreme test of levelling-down. The absolute nothing of capitalism is the "antipoint" to the "point of the new beginning!" The absolute vacuum is not a defect or deficiency of capitalism, it is its highest aim. *Capitalism is the system without Man.* All "action" now is inside of this magical, perverted "doing."

The nisus of the universe, this sublime non-demonic action is now delivered over to a demonic *doing*, which inevitably must lead to perdition and not only to *finite* death (*maveth*). Since action is today synonymous with pragmatic technical action, the Ritual consequently appears as superfluous, obsolete or superstitious. So Man is deprived of the encompassing higher spheres, the *hekhaloth*, which should surround him. The "zero-obsession" is victorious. To wrench the Ritual free from the satanic forces is the critical turning-point, and this is the grandeur of the "Now."

The failure of "doing" and the "un-do-ability" of the Ritual is not due to any hindrance from *outside*, but to our own "ritual-failure" that keeps us from sincerely and honestly adhering to it. Yet deep down it seems only too certain that Ritual is the axiom on which hinges the "to be or not to be" of Man. This means that with enlightened Man Ritual is in tragic suspension, and he waits in mortal fear. *For how long?*

Four points about the Ritual stand out:

(1) The Ritual has no "parts." It is an undivided totality-action, which is not the *sum* of various single actions. It is total-behavior. Even keeping many prescriptions can still be far from ritualistic conduct.

(2) The Ritual can penetrate in such a minute osmotic way into the body that it can affect our whole being to the deepest roots, including our physical being.

(3) Ritual is a *re-uniting* with the group. Yet when there is no gen-

uine totality, then the Ritual is like a flower cut off from the bush. Only a few small remnants of genuine groups do exist today, and they are vanishing rapidly. Genuine collectivity is nothing ethnic, cultural or political. It is "Founded People," "Israelic," "Abrahamic." But this too is in eclipse. The genuine People and the Ritual are indivisible.

(4) The regaining of the Ritual demands the ever-repeated act of the Founding of a People, because a mere belonging-together would not suffice. The *individuum* as *individual* is not ritualizable. Return (*teshuvah*) begins when the individual looks at himself as *not* only an *individual*. This is the end of absolute "privacy." Capitalism, which is fundamentally anti-communitarian, is also fundamentally anti-ritualistic.

The individual is experiencing "embracement" by virtue of his place in the People, and by looking at himself as *trans-personal*. The Ritual ascends, reaches the *word* and penetrates into the body. Man swings outwards without losing his roots. The animal's body is natural, yet takes part in the *nisus*. Man has in addition a ritual body, and this body becomes holy in the Ritual.

If the People has been lost, then the Ritual is lost and perdition (*avadon*) has come. Much harm can be done to the Ritual by perverting it through techniques and practicalism, letting it lapse into magic, instead of having it interpret, challenge and revolutionize everything else. Ritual must always overtake action, for no practical aim can replace it.

The Ritual assimilated into the corrupted sphere of action vanishes quickly. It cannot "compete." If it is built into a situation of *falsehood and untruth*, this can result only in its complete destruction. Our anguished postponement of adhering to the Ritual is the one possible answer to the self-delusion which believes that it is feasible to observe the Ritual when it is integrated into a corrupted situation. Until there is again a genuine Ritual, the Ritual-Vacuum must be kept as the constant reminder of what is missing.

Ritual is the presupposition of *doing* and *making*. Lacking it the *doing* dies. Extreme nihilism is then the only honest attitude. To act upon the unreal or the idolatrous is magic. "He who completely refrains from idolatry is called a Jew." But who can? From this Jewish doctrine everything else follows. Discarding idolatrous impurities still has to be done by the Jews. Higher spheres of purity, stripped of idolatrous impurity (*Tumah*) have to be reached.

All power necessarily leads to lunacy. But power is considered the normal method of action in our "spook-world." Ritual is Man's spontaneity in the non-magical world: "acting followed by hearing" (*naasseh* followed by *nishmah*). Resultant action derived from ideals (the Platonic pattern) is not genuine action, not an action that comes from the *primal point.*

The Ritual regained—this is the revolution of revolutions. Ritual means a Oneness, which can bring everything into motion. False action seems to promise *everything,* but in the last analysis brings nothing. Action which is merely reaction cannot overtake anything. Plato's action is contemplative, passive, looking at the prototypes: it is *Art.* The contradiction between Magic and Ritual is the everlasting antithesis in Man.

With which "reality" is the Ritual concerned? It is concerned with the Divine Call, not with "somethings." It opens up the higher, it closes down the lower; it ascends, it endows, it illuminates, but it does not "have." It is *not* of an ontic character. Although it is *confronted* it manifests itself as the challenger; in earlier times in relation to the mythos, today in relation to technical Man. But the Ritual cannot re-emerge because what it challenges now is not clearly denoted. So the Ritual seems to have been dissolved together with the mythos.

The awesome apocalyptic crisis of today is theophoric. Ritual is a *doing* that belongs to a theophoric situation and not to a man-made divided situation (*kizzutz*). It can be coordinated only to an "it-less" world and not to a demonic, magical world.

Magical action—capitalism and the technical existence that is its acme—annihilates itself dialectically. The wicked wonders of the merchandized technical world can be "salvaged" only if they are completely transformed by the Ritual. Nothing practical should ever be allowed to overtake *pure doing.*

The tragedy of the Ritual today is that it does not challenge anything. Yet the *Biblical Revolution* could undoubtably continue. The Biblical God encourages revolutions. Yes! Revolt! Against the

Nothing! Your place is not for ever and ever in the matrix, in Mother Nature! HE is the friend of the rebellious, not of the submissive. If revolution would acknowledge HIM instead of leaving HIM to re-action, light would be all around us!

Nothing now opposes our technical existence, neither capitalism nor communism. Only the Ritual can bridge the abyss between Man and the run-away technology. This gap is widening. Man has been standing still for too long. A dimly perceived Ritual-Longing for a new connection with the Ultimate seems to be coming alive. Only the trans-ontic, trans-magical, trans-cyclic can bring about an ultimate unification. Re-establish the beginning! The Ritual is the pure. primal action of Man, in contradiction to the demonic, magical action of sub-man. *Practical* action is related to perversion, brokenness and idolatrous "mirages." Violence comes from the attempt to act on these "mirages" or illusions.

One of the most damaging injuries the body can be afflicted with is the loss of the Ritual. Without the Ritual the body loses its wholeness. The whole cannot emerge above and beyond the parts as long as not *all* the parts are assembled together. The mighty realm of the body therefore is rejected. The holy body is now "matter," "stuff," "scum." It will have to be shown that the Ritual may penetrate and illuminate the body. If the body is not integrated into the Ritual, if it is for ever to be given over to the grave, then Man is lost. What should be *extran* knowledge is then only subjective and private. Biblical enlightenment includes the "holiness" of the body.

What is human in the human body has been formed by Ritual. What is animalistic in the human body may be transformed, illuminated, elevated from "matter," sanctified by Ritual. Ritual body is the way to resurrection of the dead (*tekhiyath ha metim*). A ritual body, like anything that is pure, is not "lost."

All truly noble faces are Ritual-faces, and with the loss of Ritual goes the loss of these faces. The sight of these "*un*-embraced faces" is one of the horrors of today's zero-hour. The decay of the face and the decay of the body occur because they are not ritualized.

The way is wide-open for Man, but it is one way only—an ascending to speaking and to standing upright. Israel has been established for action and cannot be affixed to fate! It does not stand

under the coercion of any natural "constellation." To continue on
its way through history means choosing that kind of "doing," which
is pure and non-magical. No secular solution such as the state, becoming "normalized," idealism or religious groupings can perpetuate
Israel's life. *Only the Ritual!* To regain the Ritual is the way *to* Life.

The Ritual is wiser than we are, wiser than practicalism. But
the new day of the Ritual has not come yet, because Ritual has not
come to grips with the passage into the technical age. Technology is
magic *returned*. Since the time Man entered into the primitive
"hunting-era," nothing of equal importance has happened up to the
"technological age" of today. A second, an even greater Biblical Revolution is imminent.

Even in Orthodoxy the Ritual so far is essentially a component
of the present situation. It is not *social*-revolutionary. To be so would
be its renaissance.

The Ritual is directed against the "powers." It brings to light a
not yet seen level-of-depth in Man.

Where then does Ascending originate, or have its roots? It originates in the latent immanence of Man, latent in all evolution. But
this latent immanent Man *is not* the natural, biological or perverted,
failing Man, but RITUALISTIC MAN! Hierarchic—vertical—elevated (*kadosh*). To *him* the cosmos is delegated, and *he has accepted*.
The nisus of nature—the hierarchy—the ascending—the upwards is
not mechanical or archetypal—it is Ritual.
In the archetypes, Man is not present, they are *pre*-human.
In the things, Man is not present, they are *sub*-human.
In the powers, Man is not present, they are *in*-human.

In the new, genuine Hierarchy nothing "collides," nothing "com-
pels," nothing "rules."

Man as the objectivated, non-magical being, is the end-product.
Making a "being" into a *thing* is the basic treason. Only Man is trans-
holistic, wholly transcendent. He is the "Ritual of the universe." He
has no "nature," only "history." Ethics is not an inner effort, it is a
Commandment . . . obeyed. It is the becoming-concrete of the
ethical.

The standards cannot be found in practicality but in the Ritual.
Yet ever again they must be renewed, not only "continued." In the

last analysis Ritual is "speaking"; it transposes the archetypes into Words. Dialogue is not yet "speaking", it is merely discussing. ("I and Thou" is not sufficient, it is *Kizzutz-born* not *Zimzum-born*.) Dialogue can remain totally inside of practicalism. Ritual is action without impurity (*tumah*), restoring our totality and purifying us.

The Ritual resembles the matrix, the "apriority of doing," from which it arises. But it is a reversal of this doing, a different attitude.

Ritualistic Man is man ordained, called upon, steered and steering! He is not aloof. Only the *Illuminated Man* is ready for this.

Ritual cannot be a thought, a feeling or a making. It is holistic, "extran." It is "public," open for all to see to an unheard-of degree. It is the strongest connection possible, nothing isolated or subjective, a collective action, free from the "PRIMAL FEAR." It is action from the "Primal-Point," not pragmatic but luminous.

Lectures / 1950-1959

Neo-Mysticism

There is a danger that something immensely important and hopeful may be missed because of the term "mysticism," a term that does not ring so nicely in our ears. The term suggests some kind of superstition, something anti-scientific, a realm of confusion or sensational secrecy. All this ruins the concept from the very beginning. But we should not miss any avenue away from Man's great anxiety, particularly that anxiety which is built on Man's loneliness, because of a questionable terminology.

What precisely is mysticism? It means a profound contemplation, a contemplation so strong that in it we become ONE with the object of our contemplation. It means a kind of fusion with the object which we are contemplating, a becoming ONE with a unity, a Oneness. And at the same time getting vistas of the whole and a new immediacy. The philosophers of mysticism are by no means confused people; they are just as clear as the greatest philosophers we know. There is nothing hazy about mysticism. Let us emphasize particularly one point: the finding of a new immediacy, a new directness. It is just this immediacy and directness which is lacking today.

There is a naive idea that understanding is—in a way—granted with knowledge. Some believe that this would be sufficient to give an ever greater chance to understand. But it is one of the experiences of our time that the more we know and the more we learn about the universe and reality, the more everything becomes mysterious. The mysterium continually deepens along with our knowledge. Our knowledge does not disperse but rather intensifies the enormous, fathomless profundity and difficulty of understanding. It is an insight of one of the great philosophers of our time, Ludwig Wittgenstein, that when we look at the simplest facts—not only at the facts we get from science, but the simplest facts of life— when we look at them with the greatest intensity, then in a way it is not possible to make them "rational." What is nearest, what is simplest, is the most mysterious.

We need to remember the timeless, the everlasting truth which is told to us in the story of the two trees in Paradise: the tree of knowledge of good and evil, and the tree of life. The Bible says that in the center, in the midst of Paradise, there was the tree of life. And there was also the tree of death, the tree of division. The fundamental idea is that Man has never touched the tree of life. We have never eaten from that tree. In modern terms it means that we wanted first to have knowledge, we wanted to know, we wanted to acquire something. There was first an acquisitional drive, and we believed that after acquisition, after security life will come. This is the fundamental illusion which is rejected in the Biblical story. What comes after we have acquired security, after we have got something, after we have transformed everything into a thing, what follows is again always a thing and not life. Life does not come. We have perverted the relation of these two possibilities. We have made a split, a cleavage between the two trees, and what we get now is merely things, but it is not life. The tree of life is no longer accessible to us. That is our actual situation. Therefore we can by no means take it for granted that by being clear, by being scientific, we also will know and understand. There is something in what is given (and it is the deepest in what is given), which is not possessional, not haveable. We have fallen into mere thingishness, into mere thinghood, and all we get is things and nothing but things.

The attitude of the mystic is an attempt to break out of this situation, to get out of this atomization, this loneliness and the nothingness surrounding us. What is here the relation of nothingness to loneliness? Where there is thingishness, where there are only things, there is loneliness because things are separated from one another. Where there is the realm of thinghood—and we are buried under-it—everything is in a state of loneliness. This is the deep root for our loneliness. Is there any way out? Have we lost the ability to overcome this situation? Walt Whitman cried out: "You are gods! You are crystalline! Your faces are radiant!" Is this so? Today we make a detour through things, tools, gadgets, psychological prerequisites, institutions, techniques. We never have any real directness. Immediacy is gone.

This is so too concerning the relation to God. Let us confront the God of the theologians with the Biblical God. The God of the theologians is a construction, something indirect. It is a Being, somewhere far away in heaven. The Biblical God is not in heaven. Although here and there something like that is said, the fundamental trend of what might be called Biblical theology, is that God is not in heaven but on earth. The consequences are far-reaching, because this establishes on earth a principle of incandescent fire, in whose nearness almost everything is burnt up if the slightest mistake is made.

The question is: Where is unity? Where is immediacy? There are two forms of unity which first have to be seen. There is a primal unity and a final unity. Primal unity means what Man had in earliest times, what is called animism. This is the idea that nothing is dead, everything is animated. Everything that surrounds us, not only plants and animals, but even stones and crystals and clouds and whatever we see, is animated and forms one great ocean of life. And to this we belong. This is the primal and original unity, a state which may be compared with that of the embryo inside of the mother. The embryo also is never surrounded by anything not alive. Man and the embryo are one and the same. We know from psychoanalysis that we have a tendency, a retrogressive tendency, to strive back to the mother, to return to that primal unity. There are great philosophies, powerful philosophies, as for instance Buddhism, which are built on this particular assumption that the highest we can reach is to go back to that primal unity from which everything has come.

All else which came later is division and finally death and meaninglessness. Only in the beginning, what Buddhists call Nirvana, is a perfect state of happiness.

But we cannot stay inside of the mother, we have to go away from her, and the history of humanity is an ever greater going away from nature. The clear diagnosis of our situation today is "a farewell to Mother Nature." We cannot stay where we have been. We have to go through history. The primal unity is lost. We have to look forward to a new unity, a new unification. Can such a new unity, a re-unification, be reached? Is it a goal which is possible? This is the problem concerning mysticism. The definition which we have given before is not sufficient—that is of mysticism as a being ONE with, a degree of immediacy. Fundamentally there are two types of mysticism—what we call *reductive mysticism* and what we call *integrative mysticism*. And these two correspond a little to the primal unity and the final unity. Reductive mysticism, which we find in the philosophies of the Far East, but not only there, has the tendency to reduce everything to the point where a uniformity is reached, the unity which is behind all things. All the differentiations, the varieties of reality are brought back to that one substance behind all things. It is a levelling, a submerging, a melting of everything into a oneness. What we see here, the variety of things, is merely a "veil of deception," as India calls it, "the veil of Maya." There always is connected with this particular form of mysticism the idea of poverty. Only when we get rid of everything, when we develop a very high degree of non-attachment, then finally we reach the point where our eyes are opened to that great unity behind all things. This is the idea of India that all separation is illusion. Ultimately all things are united. Even all of us are united ultimately. When we have the feeling that we are separated beings, this is illusion. This statement that all separation is an illusion also has a tremendous political implication.

Integrative mysticism—to contrast these two terms—is not a striving to uniformity, but to unity. Unity does not give up anything, but integrates; it keeps all the varieties, the separate reality of everything. Nothing is lost; everything is integrated into a higher unity. This is integrative mysticism. From this standpoint

an assumption is made that there is a particular place for all differences. In the concatenation of all things there is a place provided for everything, for all of us and for each of us. This unity
must include everything. For instance it must include also the dark
sides of reality. Integrative mysticism does not drop even the dark
aspects of the bodily side of existence. The greatest personification
of integrative mysticism was Jacob Boehme, a simple shoemaker,
who lived in the time of the Thirty Years War (17th century). In
his system of mysticism Boehme included also the body. Ultimately our body is holy. It can be made transparent. There is not
only the flesh but also the holy flesh. (This conception of the holy
flesh is a thoroughgoing feature of Russia's pre-revolutionary philosophy which we can find in the Russian point of view up to our
own days. To include the body, to sanctify the flesh, is a great issue
in the philosophy of Tolstoy and also—in a different sense—in
Dostoevsky and in Rozanov.)

To bring this whole pattern into modern terminology, we
have to add two more forms of mysticism: what may be called *pragmatic mysticism* and *logical mysticism*. To our amazement we find
a renascence, a re-emergence of mysticism where we might least expect it—in American philosophy. To a certain extent it can be said
that William James was a mystic. What does this mean? Here is a
great insight that cannot be attributed merely to William James, but
after all it goes to his credit that he made it perfectly clear. He
wanted to be very concrete, to get rid of all fictitious, vague, foggy
ideas. But, so William James argued, when you want to do this, when
you want to advance to an extreme degree of concreteness, there
also is an immediacy. You are not concrete when you make a detour, or derive something from other ideas, or there are intermediaries, or gadgets, or tools, or institutions. In all these there is then an
indirectness, and we are not really concrete. Nothing would be more
fallacious than the belief that we are concrete when we deal with
things. Things are very far from being concrete. Even from the
standpoint of modern science, the concept of things has completely
vanished. The so-called realistic man, who wants to stand on solid
ground, "on his own two feet", is far from being concrete. Concreteness is beyond all intermediaries. One of the fundamental fea-

tures of the Biblical conception of God is just such an absence of intermediaries. James understood that what we call things are not the ultimate reality. The true reality, which we can reach in concreteness, is immediate. When we are in an immediate relation to something, then there is nothing in-between, and no "rational explanation" is possible any longer. In each case we are confronted with an eachness, a particular situation, not a generality, a general idea. We are so near to what is concrete that nothing whatever is inbetween. There is almost a complete fusion.

This same attitude we find in some of the greatest modern painters, for instance, van Gogh. He had a strange way of contemplating things, looking at a tree or an old rickety chair, doing this for weeks and weeks and then putting it down on canvas. This is similar to what we find in Chinese paintings. The painter for a long while contemplates a certain thing—a flower, an animal, a crystal or whatever it may be. And after he has contemplated it to the point of fusion, it takes a moment only to put it on canvas or paper. We no longer have this immediacy. We continually go through detours, and we believe *things* are immediate. Things are rather something negative. A thing shows up where there is a certain hole in the social order. We could —perhaps ultimately—define things as "social holes." In modern physics we find something similar when particles are defined as "holes in nothing."

There are not two realms, James said, the one the spiritual and the other the material. He coined a brilliant parable to show this: there is a long rope and someone is pulling to one side and someone else to the other side. And this is how it is with spirit or matter. If we pull to one side, it is spirit, and if we pull to the other side, it is matter. James said that there are not two sorts of stuff. From this follows a certain attitude of immediacy and directness, in a way a new form of faith.

In "The Future of an Illusion" Freud said that religion is nothing but a childhood neurosis. If neuroses and anxieties go, religion will go also. We can, in other words, psychoanalyze religion away. This is all too true so far as almost all religions are concerned. But it may not be true concerning a certain nucleus of religion. James raised the question: Is there a religion of healthy-mindedness? Or is religion always a compensation for something that is wrong, a deficiency? In the tenth century the Jewish philosopher Saadia mentioned a few axioms or measures of what the Jewish interpretation of the Bible is. Among other things he mentioned the *directness of God*. Saadia said: God is concerned with each, with eachness. Therefore there is no general conception, no general God, no God like the absentee owner of a factory who calls up each morning and asks: "Is anything new?" Another version of the same idea is taken from a Kabbalistic text of the 13th century: "When you want to find what is the invisible, then look ever deeper and ever more lovingly into this concrete world here, and the higher world will emerge."

A fourth form of mysticism is logical mysticism. This is expressed by the same great man, Wittgenstein. It was Wittgenstein who said: "When the sense of life becomes clear to man, after long searching, then he cannot any longer say what it is." This reminds us of the *Tao Te King*, written about 500 B.C., which begins with this strange sentence: "He who knows what the Tao is, cannot say it." Tradition says that the author of the book handed it over to the keeper of the doors of the Chinese empire. Nobody had ever seen him before, and then he left and was never seen again. Wittgenstein had a clear insight that the mystical essence of our mind becomes clearer the more we are abstract. Abstract means that ultimately we can drop all pictures, even—what Wittgenstein later dropped—"logical pictures". The Bible, it must be remembered, is the magna charta which first prohibited pictures or "graven images". Pictures enslave us; they pull us down. Abstraction is pure. The higher the abstraction the more there arises a new immediacy, very different but also similar to the immediacy of James. Wittgenstein occupied the furthermost outpost we can reach. In his first book —the *Tractatus*—he said that there is no other ultimate reality or necessity but the logical. Everything outside of that is merely accidental. Continually we are here on the borderline of speech, and this book ends with these words: "Whereof one cannot speak, thereof one must be silent."

One cannot merely stop at the concreteness of the immediately given facts; facts transcend themselves. Everything in ethics, values or logic is transcending, and the entire world also transcends itself. The meaning of the world, so Wittgenstein said, must lie outside the world; it interprets the world. If we go to ever greater abstractions, we again reach the mystical.

We suffer in these days from an indirectness, from being drowned under thingishness, therefore our loneliness, our anxieties. All this disappears when we again have an immediacy—whether it is primal or final, pragmatic or logical. In all these cases we gain an immediacy which can be reached by different ways.

Finally there is a fifth form of mysticism, which we can call pseudo-mysticism. Wherever an attempt is made to fuse God and Man, the mystic wants to be drowned in God, and Man disappears like a drop in the ocean. One of the fundamental axioms of the Bible is this: there is a complete separation of God, Man and World. Man can never become God; God can never become Man. Man and God can *meet*; they are *confronted*; but they cannot *fuse*. And also—God and World cannot be fused. What must be kept separated is God, Man and World. This is a fundamental axiom for all clarity in thinking. In case this is given up, we get what rings so oddly in our ears when we say "It's mystical."

There is, however, one point which must be taken out of this pattern, and this is the fusion possible between man and man. Taking a leaf from modern physics, we can call it the Human Continuum. The continuum in physics is the unity of space and time. This is the essence of Einstein's relativity. Space and time in their togetherness show new qualities which they never had in separation. In order to join men in the Human Continuum, each individual must have reached a certain degree of completion, a certain degree of perfection. When each is a really clear person, then each is no longer private. An ultimate person is not someone who is closed-up, but someone who is wide-open. Emerson beautifully expressed this. It is nothing of a uniform collectivity, nothing of conformity. Such radical universalism can reach "a universal sympathy of all things," the realization that *all* things belong together, that they are connected with one another.

This is illustrated by a little story of Tolstoy's, "Master and Servant." Vassili, money-lover and self-lover, who has left his servant Nikita dying in a blizzard, returns, and lying on him warms him back to life, dying himself. In the following lines Tolstoy describes Vassili's thoughts as he wakes, for the last time, from his frozen sleep.

"Yes, he awoke—but awoke a very different man to what he had been when he fell asleep. He tried to rise and could not. He tried to move his leg and he could not. Then he tried to turn his head, but that also he could not do. Nikita was lying beneath him, and this Nikita was growing warm and was coming back to life. It seemed to him that he was Nikita and Nikita he, and that his life was no longer within himself but within Nikita. He strained his ears till he caught the sound of breathing—yes, the faint deep breathing of Nikita. 'Nikita is alive,' he cried to himself in triumph, 'and therefore also am I'."

This highest form of *being together* represents a genuine transcending. A new structure of reality shows up, something beyond the private "I." Our problem is where do we find a togetherness? And there is none. There are no genuine communities; there is only privacy. In the case of what we call communities they are enforced or managed or held together by superficial ties. The idea of the Human Continuum is that we meet and can only meet with other persons. With things we can have no real meeting; they have no immediacy. In the Human Continuum the one can be as the other. In the realm of thingishness, of privacy or loneliness, no fusion is possible. The higher structure of the Human Continuum is absent.

We will never see this phenomenon if we look to the politicians. In that direction there is complete emptiness; they are not in the frontlines. In the frontlines one will find strange people, the philosophers, thinkers, mathematicians. Whether based on that primal or that final mysticism, whether pragmatic or logical, this human joining shows a new structure. Let me call it a "corpus mysticum." We already begin to see it here and there faintly. It is the true and the only genuine miracle of our time. This Human Continuum, this new structure, when it does appear will have one feature, one quality: it will be indestructible. And it will be irresistible.

I finish with this quotation from Walt Whitman. "The future belongs to the radicals." He said: "Omnes, omnes (All, all). May others ignore what they may. I realize the majesty and the reality of a people en masse. And it fell upon me like a great awe. The life of the common people is the life of God. When all races, sects, classes have vanished, a genuine solidarity of MEN will emerge—a world primal again."

The New Verticality

This moment is extraordinary in the history of mankind, hardly to be compared with any previous moment, in a way "telescoping" all of them. Obviously we need a new equipment, new tools. It may be that it is possible—and this is the great hope of philosophy today—to regain the original glory of existence.

In order to understand we must not only have a mind; we also must have a heart. Also a midst, a center. But we have limbs too, we have legs to stand on, we have a head. It is this *vertical line* in Man that matters. Verticality, the upright line, is a typical Biblical conception. It is in so far different from other conceptions, that there is nothing repressive in it. Wherever we talk about systems of a higher order there goes with it a certain repressive tendency. Freud pointed out that when we want to gain something which is higher, when we want to reach a higher level, when we do not like to remain savages, we must repress the lower wild urges, but—he added—when we do repress them, we become neurotic. Therefore he confronted us with the alternative: either we remain savages, or we become neurotics. Here again we are in the realm of psychology. How can we overcome a neurosis? Let me make an attempt to show that this is a problem which touches the borderline of psychology. There is a "beyond psychology," or better let me call it "a New Beyond."

This *New Beyond* is not "extra-mundane" or outside of this

world. It is not beyond the world, but it is beyond our brokeness, beyond the split which makes us weak. This is the "New Beyond." It does not envisage a "hereafter," not an escape but an ascent. In this situation our soul is a mediator, revealing something which is deep down and something which is high above. It borders on a realm beneath, and on a realm high up. And there is a dialogue between the two realms. The present situation offers an opportunity to pierce through the bottom of the soul, and also through the ceiling. Our situation is such that our psychological problems find their solution in something which continually transcends the psychological realm.

Here is a great insight: Whatever we touch today, in the fields of research or in various fields of life, always rests on something which is not of the same character. In a way, whatever we touch—this is true too in psychology—transcends into a higher dimension. Take, for instance, matter. Matter ultimately is not something material, but underneath matter there is what we call a "mathematical matrix." Matter emerges from something which absolutely is not material, but of a mathematical character. This belongs in a way to the A B C of what Einstein said. Or, for instance, take such a statement of modern philosophy as that by Samuel Alexander. The Alexander principle was that "motion precedes matter." It, therefore, is not that motion is a movement of particles or of something material, but first there is motion and from that motion we get what we call matter.

Nothing rests upon the same nature as itself. Mathematics for instance rests upon something that is not of the same nature as mathematics. We know that there is something underlying mathematics that is not purely mathematical but of an intuitive character. Psychology also is not based on something which is psychological, but on something which transcends psychology, something trans-psychological. All our problems, private as they may be, have a root in what comes out of a long evolution, very likely of hundreds of million years. Therefore in a situation which seems to be completely personal, we find problems that may have been encountered perhaps by our ancestors millions of years ago, or even by our animal-ancestry. We carry all this in us. Freud's point is that we carry in us a tremendous amount of heredity stuff. We are a store-house of things which may have happened in the stone age, and it is dangerously active in us. Far from being bygone times, the totemistic age, the animistic age is in us in an actual way. A neurosis cannot be explained in merely individual terms. The answer, therefore, would be not so much a private, personal one, but the most general, the most universal one that we can give. The best answer, the best cure for our private perplexities goes far beyond what is private. There are, for instance, genetic conflicts, phylogenetic conflicts; there also are conflicts which have their origin in the fact that our psychological life, our soul is embedded, sandwiched in between something deep down and something high up.

When we talk about the higher up, we will be using a term of the philosopher Whitehead. He introduced the term "envelopes." They are not merely higher "floors," but each envelope is always broader than the lower, so that each one encompasses the lower. Therefore there is continually an embracing, and on each level we meet something which we do not find on the lower level. Since we also are surrounded by such envelopes, there are around us novelties which explain things and events showing up in our psychological sphere; yet they are not psychological in origin, they have their origin high up, but also deep down. It is not only that we are embracing which is lower, we also *are* embraced. And the trouble with us is that we do not allow ourselves to be embraced. We stop at the point where we are and cannot really admit, or like to admit, that there is something which embraces us. But, what embraces us, which is bigger than we are, what surrounds us, obviously is something that cannot be contained in our daily experience.

Let me say a few words about a philosopher of our time, one of the greatest of geniuses, Ludwig Wittgenstein. He published during his lifetime only one small book, a book we can compare to the profound classics of humanity. It can even be compared to the "Tao Te King," the great book of Taoism. This is by no means a superficial comparison. Wittgenstein's book is guided by principles that remind us of Taoism. He too was absolutely overwhelmed by the fact that what is the greatest insight we cannot say. And he said: "what cannot be said must be shown". And he also said if something really is shown, we cannot say it. Therefore the strange contradiction between what is known and what we can say.

Psychology is not an absolute; psychology does not stand alone. We cannot talk psychology in merely psychological terms. We must talk psychology in terms of what is beyond it, what is above it and what is underneath it. There is a principle in Hebraic thought represented by the words "The Place". *Makom* is the Hebrew word, meaning "the Place." God is called "Makom," because according to this profound insight, "HE is the Place of the World. " But the world is not HIS Place. The world in other words is not the ultimate fact, but it has *a place*.

Everything has a place. For instance, all of us have a "place" too. We cannot explain ourselves—for instance that we are here— in terms of factuality. This would be a psychological view which is too narrow. The idea that even the whole world has a place, is enlarged here or applied to each detail. A place is provided for each of us. And this place must be respected. What is wrong with us is that everybody wants to occupy the other fellow's place. Or we could also say, nothing today is standing in the place where it belongs. This is what is meant in the *correctly* translated 6th Commandment, which is not "Thou shalt not kill," but "Thou shalt not murder." The Hebrew language has different words for *to kill* and *to murder*. It says "Thou shalt not murder." And by "murder" is meant even minor acts. As a famous comment on this Commandment goes: "If you make your fellow man publicly ashamed, so that his blood rushes into his face, you have spilled his blood, you have murdered him." Why is that so? Because you have hurt his place, the place which is his legitimate place, provided for him in the concatenation of all things. This, therefore is more radical than a mere "Thou shalt not kill." Killing is not prohibited absolutely. Animals are slaughtered; there is the death penalty known in the Bible. This statement is more radical. What is wrong is that everything has been dislocated from the place where it belongs.

The Gideon Society, which distributes Bibles all over the world, has taken a sentence from The Book of Judges as a motto which it prints on all its Bibles. It is a very simple sentence: "And everybody in the camp stood in his place." And if we would enlarge this principle of "The Makom," "The Place," we can look at a sentence by a Kabbalist of the 15th century, "There where you are standing, there are all the worlds." One has not to go into the Beyond, one has not to escape from this life here. Here where you are, at this particular place, are all worlds.

When we talk, there are two directions of our speaking, not only one. Remember for a moment what we said about the envelopes. We are standing somewhere, there are envelopes below, and we look down to these envelopes. There are others, and they are higher, surrounding us. Evidently it makes a difference whether we look down or up. When we look down, there are situations which we already know. This is the definition language, and in a definition we can be very clear. However, when we use that language, what we say is a trifle. In a way, we merely label things. It does not really enlarge our knowledge. But when we are "bumping" against the higher envelope that surrounds us, then suddenly a situation is created where we are *silent*. Wittgenstein felt this in a pathetic way to such a degree that he really became silent. And only when he had discovered a certain method or a certain way to say a few words, then again did he write down a few sentences, which have been collected posthumously. These statements are among the strangest we can find. The interesting point here is that speech, true speaking, only begins when we do not merely confine ourselves to definition language. What we say then is not moonshine or non-reality; it is the true essence of language. Because of the hierarchic character of the universe, when speech reaches the point where it is exhausted and we begin to stammer and yet still speak, we need a new language which interprets the lower language.

What we indicate here about "the Makom," "the Place" is of an interpretive character. If we want to understand our psychological condition, we need also something that is bigger to interpret it, something from the next envelope. This is a conception which ultimately buttresses an optimistic view, because we are embedded in that which interprets each such lower envelope.

One of the great Hassidic leaders of earlier times was asked to tell his students something about God. And he said: I only know one thing, HE is clearly present, and besides HIM nothing is clearly present. This is an insight of an ultimate character. So when we look with the clear sharp mind of the mathematician, everything is extremely mysterious. The most miraculous things in our time are going on in mathematics. We live in a mathematical universe which —although it is clear to a certain extent—is on the other hand completely mysterious. All these equations of mathematics cannot be retranslated into the simple pictorial language of daily life. These mathematical conceptions are extremely clear, but they bring out that the simplest things that surround us are a mysterium. We are living in a deep mystery. And the greater our knowledge is, the more we learn, the more mysterious it becomes. What is quite immediate is totally mysterious. This is an insight expressed by one of the two great founders of American Pragmatism, William James. He said in effect: When you would like to become very concrete, very sober, merely in talking about what is quite immediate, it is no longer rational; the more it is immediate the more there arises a situation where you cannot say it any longer.

Speech has to be understood inside of the entire Biblical system. The word *prophet* is a Greek word, meaning "to forecast." In the Hebrew language the prophet is called "navi," which means a speaker. Nothing is said about him but—he can speak. We cannot yet speak. We perhaps stammer a little. But "the navi," he can speak. He can speak, because—this is the Biblical view—he is addressed by God and therefore has also another ability, namely to hear. For the Bible *to speak and to hear* is an indivisible unity. It is still more miserable that we hear nothing. We are in a way deaf. Our situation is not only that we are mute to a high degree, but we are almost totally deaf, nothing is coming to us. To speak is an ability that belongs to us, but it is slumbering, deteriorated, corrupted. It can be regained. What we are talking about are attempts that are made to regain what is greatest in Man. All of us—and what else can we do under the conditions that are ours—talk in the definition language. In other words, we do not really speak. We put labels on things, and that is all. Speech is a fragment in us. But we are beginning to understand what speech really means. For instance, in understanding that there is a hierarchy of languages, and each language needs another language to interpret it. It is not possible to read the Biblical text in its grandeur, if we do not understand that it is not a Book which tells us the same things we are reading each morning in the newspapers. We do not mean that it is a secret language, or a language of other-worldliness. It is an interpretive language, and therefore a true and sincere language that is not corrupted.

The greatest power, the power of thinking, is being lost now. It is also the power of making decisions. Decisions that mean a step which is irreversible. We make a decision when we make a step which changes the situation. A decision is a leap, a clear Yes and a clear No. Our Yes today is not a clear Yes, and our No is not a clear No. Where it is possible to think, to make decisions, there is speech. The attempt which Wittgenstein made is to regain speech, and to bring to our awareness that we do not clearly speak. What is going on in mathematics is indeed such an attempt to create a new pure and uncorrupted language.

The problems we suffer from, are predominantly problems rooted in the fact that we are continually ascending. We are rising from envelope to envelope, and therefore we get this strange feeling of dizziness, which is the main reason for our perplexities. Take the very high abstraction level, such as the statement: First was motion and then came matter. Or take the abstract conceptions based on Dirac's mathematics of anti-matter, that we can transform all the equations of physics, particularly of gravity, into the negative side, which is a purely mathematical operation. This was done by Dirac, and everybody said, "Well, this is only a mathematical construction." When Dirac said, let us look around, perhaps there is such a thing, *there was such a thing.* We can observe it, we even get it in little particles in our cyclotrons. Here are advances in abstraction which are enormous. All these things, however, are still relatively on solid ground, compared with what is going on now particularly in the field of cybernetics. Rightly it was said by the top mathematician in that field, Norbert Wiener, that the great invention is not the Bomb but this. Something is going on in our mind that reaches a profundity and a radicalism which surpasses everything that the wildest fantasy could imagine.

Dizziness belongs to the situation of piercing through the bottom and through the ceiling, and always reaching the border-line.

What matters is to accept this "dizziness." Again Wittgenstein had the courage to accept it. He did not make any attempt to evade it. We cannot be "contemporary people" so long as we try to evade it.

Our main sin today is that we do not ultimately accept our human destiny. Our human destiny is connected with this dizziness. We are the "principle of ascending" in the universe. We ourselves are such an envelope which surrounds nature. This is a moment when we have to understand, that we are not only part of nature, but that Man is a principle which encompasses nature. And this again is an old Biblical view. Likewise it is to a high degree suppported by advanced research, for example in biology. Man—as Julian Huxley said—is standing alone. Man is a maximal principle. Man is not one more animal. We are not a part of the universe, we are an envelope of it. That again creates a dizziness, because our relation now to nature can only be compared to the moment of birth. We are severed now from mother nature; the umbilical cord has been cut. That is the meaning of this moment. *The point here is to accept it and not to evade it.* As the French writer Albert Camus told us, there is something absurd in our life. Yet that should not make us depressed or pessimistic. Rather it is the greatness of human destiny. Man's destiny is paradoxical, and that means—in religious terms—that something extremely great is being delegated to us, not something that is "reasonable." This demand made on Man seems to be superhuman, and yet it must be accepted. It is what the great philosopher Kant called: the dignity of Man. We are looking for something petty, something practical, something to give us a shelter. We must realize that our present situation is very advanced and by no means petty. It brings us to the awareness that Man is greater than he thinks. Our ascent cannot go on if we are afraid to get dizzy.

The problems of our time are not psychological. The psychological problems, although of course we must understand them, are in a frame. There are broader problems, for instance technical ones. But if all of them were solved, the true problems still remain and they will show up then. A psychology that does not go beyond psychology is no longer sufficient. There is an opening into that which transcends the situation. *Man* is that principle—so far as we know—which closes the universe. But is this the end? No; we believe also in Man opening up a new perspective. Man is overtaking himself.

What is the limit of Man now? It is Man himself. The greatest problem today is not what is outside of us. Our problem is not the one which early Man had, being confronted with a wild hostile nature; we are surrounded by nothing but ourselves. And this is—as the advanced minds of our time see it—a much more horrible confrontation than all the horrors of nature put together. The power that comes from us is demonic to such a degree that the main problem is what we are going to do with that power. If Man were merely confined into these narrow limits and could not pierce through the bottom and the ceiling, the outlook would not be too bright. Fortunately it is not so, for we are able to transcend. We can overtake Man. This is the great hope. The answers we need are not of a private character. There are no private solutions. The answers are of a very universal character. The great cure is not my psychologist, whom I will see on Wednesday, or my psychiatrist whom I will see on Thursday. The great healer today is— great truth.

The lonely soul, the mere private soul, is unaware of the fact that it has deep roots and also wings. A soul is not alive in solitude. The solitary soul is not *really* alive. It sinks into darkness. The open soul has no longing for a life beyond, but a longing for life beyond the cleavage. We cannot go beyond the cleavage if we are merely staring into it. If we look into our brokenness, it has a paralyzing character. The more we stare, the more we try to think it over, endlessly, and in a way from a private angle, the more horrible and the more paralyzing the cleavage becomes. The split which permeates the entire universe and even us must be accepted, taken inside of us and surrounded by our human nature. This is something which only the open soul can do. That is the soul which is not sad.

Joy is not merely what we would like to have, what we may get under certain circumstances, it is *commandment*. To enjoy alone, as it is said, is sinful. The joyful soul intrinsically is not lonely. The soul of Man by its very essence is open, and this openness by its essence is joy. And more than that. It is a joy to such a degree that it is almost unbearable. It is a joy, so intense that we may rightly say: THE ESSENCE OF OUR SOUL IS JOY.

Science and Religion

Something almost miraculous is happening in our time. It is the growing harmony between science and religion. The most important things are sometimes hardly heard in the general bedlam. They are as it were whispered to us. There is something to be heard if we would listen to this secret. In the Bible it is said that God created heaven *and* earth. This points to a fundamentally great principle of unity. We must come to an ever clearer awareness of the unifications that are going on. We must have an eye very open and an ear very open to understand what is not yet visible and audible. Science and religion begin "to meet," not only to clash. So far, as we all know, there has been a burning hostility between science and religion. There were on the one hand the charges of materialism, mechanism, atheism, and on the other the charges of superstition, illusions, escapism. And no reconciliation was possible. The attack against religion was threefold: first that religion is unscientific and cannot be reconciled with scientific statements. Then came the objections from Freudian psychology, that there is nothing in religion but compensations for frailties and wishful thinking. And then the severest attack against religion: it is anti-social. It tries to cover up social injustice, suggesting that social justice is not important because everything will be straightened out in the Hereafter.

These are very severe objections against religion. And what are objections against science? Science, it is said, is a neutral aspect, an indifferent aspect of the universe; it does not know values, it only knows factualities; it is materialistic. This is another way of saying: there is no meaning in life, there is no meaning in the universe. Ideas about meaning are merely superimposed and of no scientific significance. Man does not become happier with science; Man is more and more dissolved and buried under the enormous consequences of science. Man is reduced to a mere mechanism or an animal. We want here to point to the beginning of a profound change, which is perhaps a dialectical one. In case ideas, or cultures, or attitudes are in the relation of a polarity, this is not the same as an Either-Or. In a polarity two sides go together, as the right side goes with the left, or negative electricity with positive electricity. The two are opposed, but this antagonism may be of a creative character. What is happening today is a radicalization of the true messages of science and religion. This beginning of a meeting is not the result of a watering-down of religion or of science, but of a very profound radicalization, illustrating the principle often seen today: that only where ideas are radicalized are they able to touch one another. Something like this is going on in science and religion. Both begin to overtake the present situation, the present problems—for instance the perplexities stemming from technical existence, from our being buried under the results of science and technology. The insight is dawning that our deepest problems, the true human problems, are not practical problems or "how to 's." They are scientific, they are not of an organizational character. The human problems cannot be solved in a practical way.

Audacious steps are made by religion and by science, and both show us ever clearer the essence of what they are. Both are discarding old fallacies too, both are maturing. They make not only a harmony, which would mean a mere getting along with each other, not a cooperation, but a dialectical polarity.

A few words about science. What has changed in science? We can understand the general point of view of science that anything in the other camp is simply superstition. But that is changing. Since Darwin our ideas about evolution, for example, are different. Darwin talked about causes, but not about purposes. Strangely enough, the author and father of the theory of evolution was looking backwards, from where everything comes. Each step of evolution causes the next step, and to talk about purposes was merely superstition. There are no purposes, there is only causality. Sociologists today tend to be emergent-evolutionists. This means in evolution something new shows up. From where does it come? This can be understood when we do not solely look where evolution is coming from, but also where it is going to. We speak today about tele-finalism, *the tendency, the direction of evolution.* There is a telos, an aim, a goal. Therefore one of the main issues, which divided people at that time, no longer exists.

Today we also talk about the *evolution of evolution.* This means, there is not merely an evolution, which is going on from step to step, comparable to a staircase, but rather an evolution which is ascending and is better compared to an escalator. The entire staircase is rising. This is what we believe today. Evolution as such is undergoing an evolution. The methods, if we may say so, the structure of evolution, undergoes an evolution too.

One of the most important issues which divided people has completely vanished. There are no longer in evolution merely *resultants,* or things that are merely the consequence of previous stages. When we talk about emergent evolution, this means something shows up which was not in the previous situation. William James said that the universe contains genuine novelties. It is not finished. We do not live in a block-universe but in an open, a pluralistic universe. When you deny this, you abolish the fundamental principle on which this country is constructed. There are emergents, there are also submergents. Continually something is also discarded and thrown out. And this too changes the situation definitely, profoundly.

At all times we had different ideas about the question of heredity. There was a great discovery made by Weissman shortly after Darwin, that acquired properties, or properties we acquire in our lifetime, do not go over by heredity to the next generation. The idea that the channels of heredity are too narrow and do not carry any progress, is one of the objections which the idea of evolution had to face. But there is a holistic transmission, which means that the totality, the wholeness of evolution is present in each moment.

Let me use a comparison. It is as if we see in a building in construction, from beginning to end, the blueprint of the architect. The blueprint of the building as a whole is present every moment. Otherwise no step can be made.

There was on the side of religion an old fundamental question. The question was: are we, each of us as individuals, merely products of the parents, nothing but the parents, as it were "reshuffled"? Or is there something in us that is new? In the terminology of religion, resultant evolution was called *traducianism*. Traducianism taught that we are merely the parents reshuffled. *Creationism* on the other hand believed that, of course, to a very high degree we *are* the products of the parents, but there is in each of us a spark which was not in the parents, a genuine novelty in each of us. Exactly this was the idea of the Bible. There is something absolutely new in each of us, which is added to that which we get from the parents by heredity.

There is an enormous upsurge in nature, a tremendous rising. Let me quote here Samuel Alexander, who—in one of his most important books—made this statement: that if he did nothing but look at this upsurge in nature, this continuous rising and rising ever higher, it would make him a religious person. There is however an end, a definite end of this upsurge. In a way it has ended with Man. All nature seems to be running into Man. We are coming together, all trends are coming together, collected and focused in Man. But this does not mean that the upsurge has completely vanished. It is rather delegated to us. What had been done by nature, has now to be done by us. Although the improvements which parents have acquired do not go over by heredity, they can go over by teaching. Therefore, the next generation does not get everything just without any effort. This is the fundamental change. Where this enormous rising of nature has disappeared, something is introduced by us, voluntarily, and this is done by the religions. What is no longer done for us by nature, is now done by the religious rituals. There is unfortunately a complete decay of rituals, and as it seems to us, in this we are touching on the main points of the decadence in our situation.

Perhaps in a nutshell we could say: there is a clear tendency to re-enthrone Man. This was exactly the issue when science and religion clashed at the time of the Tennessee trial, because the idea was, Man is nothing but an animal. This was what the scientists said. And the religious camp said Man has been created in the Divine Image. Of course the one could not understand the other. The question was, is Man different from the animal in degree or in kind? The answer modern biology is giving is that we are different in kind, not only in degree. Therefore it is not denied that there is a relation between Man and animal, but it is denied that it is a "gradual" one. One could pile up an enormous numbers of features to show us scientifically that there is a difference *in kind*. Let us pick out one feature. According to modern biologists, all living beings develop to a certain degree, then reach a certain perfection, and this is then the end. All these ways are being closed one after the other. There is no one way open any longer, biologically, where progress or evolution could go on.

Whitehead, who was not only a great philosopher but also a great scientist and mathematician believed that the entire universe has an hierarchic character. It is not all on the same level, simply material but it has layers, and the one envelops the other. This means that Man is a structure which encompasses the lower level. Man therefore is not one little item—perhaps a very insignicfiant one—in the infinitude of the universe, Man is the trunk of the biological tree, a principle which is broader than all the other principles we know. There is a cumulative character in this higher structure. Continually something is added, something which is new and cannot be reduced to lower levels. Once a level has been reached, it does not sink back to the lower levels. There is an autonomy, *fields,* and each such level or envelope perpetually makes a declaration of independence to the lower level. Whitehead said this is a universe which preserves values.

We know from great discoveries in science that nature is not infinite, nature is finite. This is a conclusion which comes from the great discovery called entropy. This discovery made decades ago by Clausius and Carnot, is that the universe is running down, like a clockwork. Einstein's universe too is finite. It is not that nature has existed and will never cease to exist, whatever its particular shape or form may be, but it has a beginning and will have an end. There is no difficulty to see that here religion and science meet. Nature, the universe, is a drama, which has to fulfill its purpose. In the Biblical expression, nature has been created. In other words there is nothing which carries its essence in itself. Reality is bestowed and it can be taken away.

Now we say it in scientific terms. We will not meet anything in the universe, in the galaxies or in the tiniest inside of the atom, which is not relative. Nowhere in nature do we meet anything which is absolute. And here is a still broader point, where there is a very profound coming together. Listen to our physicists, to our mathematicians, everything that they talk about is abstract to the utmost. For instance, everything which is material has completely vanished. Matter does not exist in modern physics; it is not what we would call *motion*, a movement of a body or of particles. *Motion is something entirely abstract.* No matter is needed in motion; there is nothing which moves. For example, Schroedinger's famous wave-theory describes a completely immaterial motion. Matter has disappeared. Force has disappeared. The idea of causality is undermined by *quantum-theory* (Planck). Everything that would enable us to get some kind of picture of the universe has vanished. The ultimate particles are very strange entities. But much more important is the definition which has been given by the physicist Dirac and was accepted by so great a man as Eddington, that these which we call particles are not something but are "holes." As a comparison: In the aquarium we see—to provide air for the fish—bubbles which rise up in the water. The bubbles are air, but what we call particles are merely holes. We may say "holes in what?" Let me quote a statement made by Eddington who said that the particles are "holes in nothing." The astronomer Sir James Jeans said, the universe is concretized mathematics. *The universe we live in is not pictorial.* In this situation there is no picture, and more than that, we know now for sure there will never be a picture of the universe again.

What has this to do with the religious point of view? It is connected with the prohibition of images, which you will find in the First of the Ten Commandments. There are many inconsistencies later on, but fundamentally all pictures are taboo in the Bible. No picture whatsoever can stand for any reality. This is the implication of what the Bible said and this is what we will find in advanced science. There is between the universe and the highest abstractions a mighty kinship. Einstein said that the greatest miracle is that we can understand a little bit of the universe. How is this possible? Merely because the universe and our minds have something in common. The situation is not that the universe and the mind can never reach the other, but rather that they are in a way made of the same stuff.

Our method now is not merely to look around and see what we can observe, and then try to explain this theoretically, but to reverse the situation; first think, and that may take us to a point from which we get a certain view and see things which we never could discover by mere observation, even if we would observe for tens of thousands of years. Therefore there is a primacy of thinking, enabling us to observe things that we could not see without that particular act of thinking. Materialism is here not rejected merely for religious reasons; materialism exists only as a practical attitude in our life; but as a theory or philosophy it is completely dead. Materialism does no longer exist; it is being removed by science.

What has changed in religion? In religion we find a total decline of mythology. Religion has the accent on what is ethical, and not on what is cosmological. In religion there is no longer a particular cosmology that we could pick out of these endless patterns which are offered down the millennia. The essential thing is something that is ethical, what should be done. This is a point which was emphasized to the utmost by one of the greatest of philosophers, Kant, when he said that the essence of things is in ethics and not in metaphysics. The universe is an ethical universe, not a metaphysical or physical-psychological universe. Pascal, who looked at the universe from a religious point of view and also as a great mathematician and scientist, made this statement: "God no longer gives signs from the cosmos." To a certain extent the universe is silent. Pascal, looking at the stars, said: "This silence, this eternal silence frightens me." A very great statement. There are no longer direct signs. Again, this has something to do with a fundamental fact, and without understanding it nobody can be a contemporary person—namely, that the abstraction level is continually rising, while the pictorial level is continually sinking. And this is in the awareness of religion too. True religion has nothing to do with mythology, with cosmological insights. The Bible is not a textbook of cosmology. That is a naive approach to discuss the Bible as if it were an old-fashioned textbook of physics, which no longer fits into our times. Religion shows a much more important side. Religion (and we talk now about advanced religion) can no longer be a servant of institutions, classes, churches or interest groups. Religion in reality is just the opposite of this. Instead of buttressing and protecting injustice, superstition or backward conditions, in its very essence it is rebellious.

The essence of what the Bible did was not to give convenient answers to our problems. The Bible did not come and tell us, "Here are the answers to our problems, to the perplexities and enigmas which face us, and now we can get peace of mind." Instead the Bible stirred up unrest. The entire ethical realm, which is hardly detected and dealt with, has suddenly become a mighty issue. What the Bible did to humanity was that it made an end to the hundreds of thousands of years of prehistory, and started history with all the unrest we must go through. It will be unrest, it will be conflict, but we must not retreat and try to make a short-circuit and go around this, because the true answer will be at the end, when we have gone through history, and not before that. The monotheistic concept of the Bible, the idea of God, is a challenge which makes life almost unbearable. Because HE showed up in the Biblical text not as a convenient nice answer or as an old gentleman. HE showed up in the Bible as a consuming fire. If we would make an ever so tiny mistake, a tiny ritual mistake, we would be burnt up.

What matters is that true conception. Why is this so alien to us? There is a very simple answer. Because our actual situation is such that this idea of Biblical monotheism cannot be projected onto the level on which we are living. It is not—as many people believe —that Nietzsche was right when he proclaimed in his "Gay Message": "God is dead. Don't you know this yet, we have killed Him." It is not that God is dead, but that the levels we are living on are dead. They are not theophanic any longer.

We want to bring out the idea of Biblical radicalism. This

would be a situation no longer vulnerable to the three objections we have mentioned: that religion is anti-scientific, merely an escape and a sublimation for our frailties. Or that religion has as its only purpose to belittle life, to belittle social chaos, and to teach that everything will be straightened out in the Hereafter. These arguments have gone. We will notice that the Book of Job already made this point. It said, when the three friends came to console the man who was so horribly tested and asked "where is justice," the three friends offered exactly these consolations. The mighty answer of the Book of Job is: Man is uplifted from the cosmological level. Not Man any longer questions God, "Where is Thy justice?" but God questions Man: "Where wast thou when I created the universe?" Man is on a level, where Man does not belong. And it cannot be expected that justice ever will come on that level.

When we detach ourselves from the people we also lose all the forms of what is called the Ritual, and we end in a mere spiritualism. We would believe that all the answers are outside of the concrete world, in a Beyond or a Hereafter. Such a religion of spirituality, or other-worldliness is a teaching which we still find even today. Inside of history it is said nothing ever can happen which is essential. Therefore no Messianic change is possible, but only eschatological change. Messianic change also would bring history to an end, but *inside* of history, when history is fulfilled, not because history has been given up or has been evaded. Exodus means, not a going away from one place to another, but what we call a *vertical* exodus. Science has risen and matured immensely and so has religion. Religion is no longer the old consolation-system, but a great challenge. Let me here mention a very beautiful statement by Franz Kafka: "The trouble with me is not that I am closed into the world and cannot get out of it, but that I am locked out and cannot get in." This is the true religious attitude. We want to get in into the *mysterium magnum* of the world. And science no longer is a devaluation of life; life is no longer reduced to a mere mechanical process. Science today makes the universe transparent. The greater science is, the greater our progress, the deeper is the mystery. The universe shows ever deeper sides, it is not flattened out into a dead meaningless machinery; it now shows up as the *mysterium magnum* of fathomless profundity. The more we know the greater is the mystery. Science and religion affirm each other. They even are enhancing each other. Each intensifies the other. *In the beginning God created heaven and earth,* not one *or* the other. Therefore it is a true prophesy, that greater than the first miracle—namely the one of creation—will be the last miracle.

Let me finally mention these conclusions, concerning the relations of science and technology and, on the other hand, religion. It is not possible to stop science and technology. We have squarely to face the fact that we only are at the beginning of the technical revolution, which will transcend even the boldest imagination. It is even not desirable to try to stop it. Because what is science? Science and technology are our superiority over nature. They are our rulership over nature. In this we are establishing our fundamental destiny, to be the binders and rulers of everything which is in nature. And then what is the hope? The hope is this: that the secrets which the universe reveals to us, are not revealed to demons, but to humans. All our perplexities would at this same moment disappear, and we would be able to administer science, and to live with science and technology. How can we be human without having these great, ultimate, mighty goals, which true religion shows? There is nothing to prevent accepting science and technology, and yet being—in a modern sense—religious.

Let me end here with a few beautiful words by Walt Whitman:

> Nobody was half devout enough, nobody yet has
> worshipped half enough, nobody knows how divine
> he is, and how certain the future is.

May we say: Man is greater than he thinks.

Essays on Judaism / 1933-1956

The Place of Nature*

Great problems do not permit of being *solved*. The greater a problem, the more it is necessary to grow out of and beyond it. Problems are conflicts which require growth concurrent with them, that
they may surpass their plane; they cannot be dealt with by question
and answer. Those who dispute about a problem are fighting usually
on the same plane and merely confront the problems from diverse
sides. Problems are tensions arising out of growth on to a higher
plane. Therefore, as Kant most truly said, it is "of all things the most
difficult to know what can reasonably be asked." The highest problems of mankind are not settled by discussion but by world-history
itself. They are the *theme* of world-history.

A fundamental error in the attitude of mankind towards the
great questions of existence lies in the belief that an autonomy may
be set up within the ambit of every problem. Thus, questions
arising out of physics are believed to be answerable in purely physical terms. Or it is believed that questions arising out of economics may be solved by purely economic methods. The truth is that all
great questions form a unity and the answers come about through
an ever larger and wider-embracing integration of provinces often
lying far apart from one another. In each case a step must be made
to a higher dimension. For example, the great questions of physics

* The quotation marks and capital letters used in the original printing (*Purpose*,
Vol. 5, 1933) have been retained in this printing.

were first brought to more sound solution when the phenomena in our three-dimensional space came to be regarded as a simplified shadow-picture of events in a world of a much higher number of dimensions. Thus the terrible entanglements of our times, the political and industrial convulsions, will hardly be capable of solution unless we grow beyond them by an integration of these provinces with other provinces which do not directly pertain to economics and to politics. Such a province is the relation of Man to Nature.

The relationship of Man to Nature has come today to a critical point. Man has been seized by fear that he has receded too far from Nature. Man is asking himself whether the path of emancipation from Nature has been the right one or whether he has been on the wrong track; on a path which leads to an abyss or perhaps to a blind alley. Should this fateful path be followed still further? What will happen if Man continues his emancipation from Nature? Will not Man then become bloodless, weak, uncertain, lacking in instinct? Will not Man, as Nietszche so greatly feared, become decadent? Will he not become an "asphalt-man," an under-man, consumed by resentment? A pure brain-man without magic strength? Many philosophers have already challenged this increasing "bloodlessness" and uprooting of Man, confronting him with his original force whilst he was still chained in Nature? The philosophy of clinging to the earth, of the glorification of the thrust of animal forces, defies the spirit of Man. "The Spirit as Antagonist to the Soul" is the title of the main work of Klages, a representative of all those tendencies which regard the emancipation of Man from Nature as a catastrophe. The truth is that such an attitude results eventually in the denial of Man's real nature, for the essential distinction of Man is precisely the fact that he is not merely a part of Nature but that he constitutes a point at which existence transcends the ordinary conception of Nature.

There are indeed two opposed and fundamental conceptions: the one sees Man as a piece of Nature, a minute wheel in the infinite wheel-work of Nature, a subsidiary product of Nature which perhaps may even be regarded as dispensable—perhaps even a mistake of Nature; a sort of appendix of Nature which might endanger and damage the whole of Nature, better cut away for the benefit of Nature! For this Man eventually threatens to damage and to use up the whole of Nature.

There is another conception according to which Man has a specific existence which is distinct from Nature in principle. The "being" of Man is fundamentally different from the "being" of an animal or a plant, and again these are different from the "being" of a mineral. Accordingly there is not a general "being" in which all inanimate things, animals and Man take part in a similar way, so that what they have in common is existence. But it is the differentiation of existence that is fundamental, the concrete "being," whereas such a general notion as "existence" is an abstraction.

The whole of Nature is constituted around Man. Man is the center of Nature; Man is the keystone of Nature. Without this keystone the whole edifice of Nature would collapse just like a dome without its keystone. Man is the building-plan of Nature and is implanted therein as her secret. The profusion of the forms of Nature cannot be explained by Nature itself but by this mysterious center, revealing a higher plan which surpasses Nature and indicates the true meaning of all its evolutionary progression. The things of Nature, plants, animals, are the objective manifestations of the path along which Man has passed through the aeons. Man appears last of all as the plan of a building becomes wholly visible only when the work of building is complete, although it was the pre-condition of building. What in purport was first becomes perceptible last.

There are, therefore, two irreconcilable conceptions, diametrically opposed, and it is clear that the conflicts of our time cannot be surmounted so long as Man fails to choose between these two. For without a decision there is no going on. This paralysis of indecision causes the real fearfulness of our time. That there is manifold change is not terrible, neither that the old dies, nor that the new comes. This sustained standing-still—that only is terrible. In the sphere of this problem lies hidden the key to conflicts of a wholly different kind, the key to the political and social conflicts, the solution of which depends on that decision. The fearfulness of this moment resides in the fact that Man has been horrified at having to part from the great Mother Nature; he is like a child which, left alone for the first time by its mother, fearfully tries to return to her. Another picture: It is the hour of birth and the severance of the navel-cord: a moment which is a shock from which no one is ever freed throughout the whole of his life—the birth-trauma. Yet a birth not carried through means the death of mother and child.

Man is infantile. His fear of the World makes him ever more unwilling to part from Mother Nature. He is full of desire to remain with this Mother and not to start on his way in the world. In this hesitation lies the main cause of the unsolved situation of our times. The path which should have led away from Nature, and had hardly been started upon, is already being abandoned again. The path is declared to be a wrong one although only the first hesitating steps have been taken along it. It is quite impossible to decide in advance whether this path leads to a catastrophe or into a blind alley. That cannot be decided by discussion but only through experience. Man who is emancipating himself from Nature seems weak, decadent and without instinct because he has remained stranded in the first germinating beginnings. He remains in an unliberated, infantile stage in which the possibilities of his real existence have not yet been manifested.

The immense movements of our time which are termed "reactionary," are attempts to make Man the servant of Nature. They are fixed on ideas such as attachment to the soil, nationality, peasantry, race. All these ideas emanated from the same basic motive, that Man remains submerged in Nature. The resentment of Man the clod, rooted permanently in the earth, of the peasant in his opposition to the man of the town, is the struggle between Man subjected to Nature, infantile Man, and those who have "come to" a human autonomy, released from the daemon of Nature. This antithesis is the real theme of world-history. On the earth, not on Man, lies the curse. The conception of an Original Sin, which puts *Man* under a curse, is a falsification of the great and profound Biblical teaching. There it stands in clear words that the curse of God was on the earth. It is not written that the freedom of Man is infringed by fate.

Why is naturalism infantile? In the Biblical text there is a phrase, one of the greatest ever uttered on earth. It is found in the first command of the Decalogue. It is the sentence: "Thou shalt not make unto thee any graven images . . ." These words are actually the real measuring-rod of humanity. "*Any* graven image," not only of God but also not of Nature's things, "or any likeness of any thing that is in heaven above, or that is in the earth beneath, or that is in the water under the earth." This highly strange demand has been hardly observed outside the Jewish and the Moslem faiths. Only today has this teaching an obedient follower: modern physics. For the first time in his history Man makes for himself no image of Nature.

All conceptions of Nature from ancient times up to our days are images. The image of the earth as of a disc surrounded by a world stream, over-canopied by the bell of the heavens; or of the earth resting on an elephant which stands on a tortoise; or the spheres of the world of the middle-ages with Heaven and Hell as Dante conceived them; or the Crystal Spheres of the school of Pythagoras, or the later astronomical systems. Even the conception of molecules and atoms, of the smallest corpuscles which are in contact and movement with one another, all these are in the nature of images and easily imaginable for everyone, even for a school child.

Only modern physics has banished all imagery from its province. The theory of Relativity, the present rendering of Nature in terms of mathematics, cannot be conceived in images, not because it is so difficult but because in principle it cannot be so rendered. There is no possibility to re-translate the mathematical symbols and the formulae of modern physics into images. The reason is that modern physics no longer works with the hypothesis of all images, namely, three-dimensional space. But rather with a space which is welded with Time as a fourth dimension into a "continuum." Modern physics even allows this space to be bent as a surface may be bent, and it finally allows this space more than three dimensions, even numerous dimensions. Space and Time are no longer empty and neutral containers in which events happen, but are welded with the event to a unity. Space and Time, therefore, can no longer be a measuring-rod with which the event is measured, but they reside in the event, in its center, and they change with the event. By virtue of the art of the modern manifold-dimensional mathematics, Space and Time change always according to the character of the event. Natural phenomena reside no longer in Space and Time, but Space and Time in natural phenomena. Consequently, all absolute standards have been destroyed. It is clear that such a conception must remain fundamentally without imagery. No image can be made of this mathematical Nature.

But what signifies then *that* Nature of which an image can be made, the Nature in which we live, the Nature in which the sun shines and winds blow and the flowers smell sweet? That Nature is a world of images. What is a world of images? A world of images is a childlike world absorbed in itself. It is the world of mythology. Mythos signifies the deification of Nature. Mythos means polytheism. In the imageless world of modern physics all is relative and nothing has absolute existence; nothing lives from itself, there is only relationship. In the world of images, in the world of Mythos, everything has substance, everything lives its own life. The world of modern physics is dead and the world of Mythos, the world of images, alive. But this alive-ness is an illusion.

To perceive this is exceedingly difficult. One of the greatest scholars, Bachofen, penetrated into this already far-sunk world of images. Bachofen started out with the question: What gave the men of antiquity such remarkable composure towards death? And the answer was that antique man still lived in the world of images, in which really there is no death at all, because it is a world of constant change, where there is nothing but that which changes. It is a world animated by ghosts, not a world consisting of indifferent matter. Bachofen says, it is "hetaerische Vermischung," a lust for self-destruction and transformation.

But if there is no death in that kingdom, there is therein also no real life. To life belongs precisely the struggle in the world, the free spontaneous resolve, and not merely the state of drifting along. In the world of images there is no anxiety; nothing is pushed aside, everything flows limitless into everything else. In our world, the world of today's realities, one thing pushes another, everything is full of danger. Everything depends on initiative and the whole bane of this world resides in the fact that everything is vulnerable, that therein hunger, thirst and drift hold sway. For only through all these factors does the world open out. The world of images is without Ethos, not objective, but concerned only with itself; ours swings out beyond itself, away from itself, and therefore it is objective. This is the antithesis of image and word. The image dreams; the word speaks. Speech is the most supreme phenomenon of all phenomena on earth. In speech Man manifests himself. But in the world of imagery he remains closed up. That childlike state leads to childishness and if it persists to perversity. Of incomparable profundity is the conception that the world emerges from the Word. In this great vision the first creation is of Light. Herein is the Scripture in complete conformity with modern physics, which also accepts light as the standard and basic principle of physical events. But before Light the Word already exists. Out of the Word breaks forth Light. Man's way of emancipation leads from image to word. Man speaks. Speaking Man is Man manifested. Man of the image-world is closed up, a dead man, a pre-man, yet it is indeed a magic world of seductive power, peopled with phantoms, a fairy-tale as opposed to reality. But only in reality, not in a fairy-tale, is made possible the meeting of Man with the Absolute.

The world of images is not only childlike, it also is perverted. We know from psychoanalysis that childhood, more especially earliest infancy, is beset with perversions, more weighty than the perversions of later life. It is a fundamental error to believe that the early is the natural and the good world. The perversion of that early stage lies in the fact that Nature then was conceived as independent and as being in itself an absolute reality. Nature is not a "pure" beginning, but is always in a condition of being destroyed, of sinking away. Nature is not "natural" but perverse when she does not occupy the place which belongs to her, namely below Man.

Nature is passive. Nature is created; it is a creature. Nature is material which should be taken up by men to be transformed into pure activity. Instead of Nature yielding to Man, Man has subjected himself to Nature. Man has perverted his free spontaneity to a passive submergence in Nature. As a result, the whole of Nature has been violated and dragged down by men into perversion. What stands before us as Nature is not Nature but a distorted image, an expression of Man's own perversion. It is the expression of Man's great fear of his own task: to bring life into the world and so build up a "living" world. Wherein lies the distinction between Nature and World? World is Nature with Man at the center. Nature without Man as keystone and center is daemonic, without ethics. Ethics is the law of the human world. It is a terrible error to believe that Man can be healed by "surrender to Nature." The whole of Nature is pervaded by death, each devouring the other. Modern physics is so great—and our times would have greatness if they contained nothing else than this physics—because it is free from every mythological and daemonic element. The inability to render the modern conception of Nature in imagery and as having life in itself signifies the triumph over daemonic impediments.

All conceptions, all social structures which are characterized by soil, race, or biological elements, are doomed inevitably to sink back to the daemonic. Therefore, there can be no conciliation between nations, but at the best an armistice. For nations are bound up with the soil, natural and biological phenomena. They have grown—like trees, like rocks, like animals. But everything human is consciously established. That it is intended and not achieved in Nature's way is not its weakness but its strength. The cause of our weakness is the fear of achieving the highest form of initiative, not the withdrawal from Nature. Only a definite supercession of Nature, a resolute abandonment of fetishes, can bring about a conciliation. Only in a purely human world, not in a world half-human, half-daemonic, is peace possible.

The great pronouncement: "Thou shalt not make unto thee any graven image" dealt with the old magical and mythological worlds for all time. Nevertheless the magic and mythological powers carry-on a ghostlike existence in our souls. They are by no means subdued. In the progress of history they have been revived in the great philosophic systems. One of the earliest endeavours to overcome mythology was the Totem cult—that tremendous attempt to bind the animal-elements in Man; the animal as the tribal-father of a tribe, of a group, of a clan! This signifies an objective discrimination of animal characteristics; a state of opposition to the natural, contrasted with the animistic early times where Man and animal were bound up in one stream of being. Here begins an initiative, although of a magical type, which divides Man from his animal basis. At this point starts a determined emancipation. The natural in Man becomes the material capable of transformation. The process develops in sacrificial rites and rituals; and at a later stage into myths and ideo-religions, though streaked with perversions. This gigantic process is far from being ended. In the struggle of emancipation, by means of the totem, man strangled himself. And the main step remains to be taken—the step from those phases which represent the embryonic life of mankind to the birth of mankind.

In those early times came also the invention of the mask. The mask is one of the greatest inventions of the human mind. In the mask, Man cleaves himself into a twofold existence. Side by side with his own being he plays a second role. This splitting up, this schizophrenia is one of the earliest separations between Man and Nature. At a later stage Plato took up again the old mythological thought and gave it the form which has influenced Europe up to the present day. Plato took over from the old mystery cults the basic idea of ancient magic: that the *image* has more reality than the actual, accidental thing. The *original image* of the tree is more real than this accidental tree here in the garden. The world of original images is slowly transformed by Plato to the world of Ideas. The transformation process was completed by Aristotle. Here the Ideas have become general concepts, the so-called "Universals," from which the basis of the dualistic conception of the Middle Ages derived. In later philosophies, in Kant and especially in his follower, Fichte, the domination of Nature is almost eliminated; it has dwindled down to an enigmatical residue but in principle has not been overcome. The reason is that, particularly in the German idealist philosophy, everything is reduced to Man as an abstract subject, not to Man in the concrete. Western philosophy invariably remained under the spell of the abstract images or ideas of Platonism. A process of transcendentalism was followed instead of one of integration. The problem forced upon us by Nature was avoided, instead of Nature taking its proper place in relation to Man, instead of its being assimilated and, as it were, eaten up and transformed like nourishment. This whole development of idealism flows into subjectivism. The latter, however, was not capable of overcoming our problem with Nature. The subject was isolated and shut in. For the subjugation of Nature can only proceed from a system and a structure greater than Nature: that is Man self-revealed. The self-revealed Man is he who has speech, that is Social Man. Social Man lives in community, in which nothing is any longer merely determined naturally. The whole of Nature therein is only a moment just as a line is only a moment on a surface, as a surface is only a moment on a body.

To establish such a world of Man signifies the energetic striding forward away from a world determined by Nature. This world of Man has not yet appeared. Man faced with this possibility is still like a child that does not know what to make of it. The obstructive movements in this dangerous hour are obviously attempts to hold fast again, if only for a moment, to the infantile state of being bound to the mother. All this is a last flicker of the old magical, mythological worlds before they completely die out. Such is the meaning of the present crisis, which carries with it the danger of becoming a cataclysm. It signifies a crisis which can end in extinction. Man—falling back under the fetters of naturalism—might lose a last decisive battle. Never yet has the danger been so great for Mankind as it is today.

Dispersion and Reunification

JEW—this means an ever growing tension of life through an ever greater concern with the world and an ever greater joy of being in the world. Thus, Jewishness comes closer to reality, but also becomes more difficult. A new turning point is imminent for Judaism. An hour of decision: either a continuation of the way through history on an ever higher level or extinction!

The primary danger does not come from outside, even though many afflictions are being visited on the Jews. Yet these attacks have never done irreparable damage to the Jews. Even the most massive onslaughts could not subdue them. The mightiest powers in history have come to naught on that rock. The more basic danger lies inside, and there is only one such: assimilation. The old questions remain: Why be a Jew? Is Judaism still necessary? Is Judaism still possible?

Asking these questions is already a fundamental misunderstanding of Judaism. To be a Jew—that is a reality, not something one can "become," or "get rid of." The Jew cannot strip himself of Judaism, he can only hide it. It can corrode or wither, but it will remain Judaism. "Assimilation" means lowering one's own pattern and falling back into outgrown stages. To prohibit such a regression is a principle of the Jewish tradition. In that tradition each stage of development must be sealed off from the lower ones, somewhat as meat is sealed off from milk, or the systems of motion and muscles from the system of glands and sex. To be the standard-bearer for this proscribing of regressions is the meaning of a "chosen people," a "Holy People." "Holy" connotes being set apart, elevated, lifted out of the chaos, blocked off from illusion and perversions.

Since Judaism is an actuality and not something that can be put on or taken off as we please, it is a reality from which there is no escape. It is not the same as the seeming reality of nations, because it has been brought about by an utterly profound decision, by a transformation. It is a reality that has been "founded." However, a soul, "rooted out from the people" dies in the deepest sense of the word. It is extinguished.

Assimilation or paralysis! Both come from the same root: Forgotten memories of the essentials of our being! Every renascence was born of an enormous onrush of memory. Our genesis suddenly becomes present; again we choose and accept our destiny. And that is the essence of "character"—to accept one's destiny and to transform it into freedom.

It is said: "Jerusalem was destroyed because the letters were not clearly pronounced." This profound saying that decadence starts with language shows how imperceptibly decline begins. The character of a people becomes blurred and indistinct as it drops from the consecrated heights of Living. The center then cannot keep its hold on the outer reaches of the people. With assimilation the connection between the center and the daily life is lost. This in turn has a paralyzing effect on the center, and that which stabilizes the continuity of the Jewish people throughout the millennia stagnates and declines. It is a vicious circle, ending in the belief that Judaism is "obsolete." A fathomless knowledge is lost and with it the profound joy and the insight that Judaism is the furthermost front and not backwardness.

The "eternity of the Jewish people" is not the eternity of a mummy. The "golden chain of tradition" does not pass on our wisdom or our profound destiny like a time-worn ornament inherited from generation to generation. Israel, which is not a country or a nation, but the Jews wherever they are, means not only rising higher, but rising higher ever and again. To stand still is already a regression. The Torah is not a manual of dogmas and prescriptions. It is the record of the founding of the Jewish people. Our great sage Jehuda Halevy said the Jewish people is the heart of mankind, mankind in miniature. Thus the founding of the Jewish people fulfilled the pre-requisite for becoming universally paradigmatic because its teachings were so closely intertwined with living events. They are not abstract dogmas as in the other religions.

For the Jewish people a serious task was ever present. They had to enunciate over and over again the meaning of their tradition and live it afresh in each moment of fleeting time. When it was done insufficiently or inaccurately, the people's life withered away, there was hardly a living Judaism. If the chain of tradition were ever to be *completely* broken, the Jewish people would die. "The heart of mankind" would stop beating. The eternity of the Jewish people does not guarantee perpetuation but means that its essence is inexhaustible. One can, however, deny or reject one's essence, just as one also can voluntarily affirm it. "The golden chain," which connects the beginning and the end—"creation" and the "world to come"—can break.

Man is in great danger! The Jews are in great danger! Noah is said to have been ridiculed when he predicted the destruction. Anyone who ridicules the prediction of a new cataclysm does not understand the decisiveness of this moment. This moment is not merely a *crisis*. Mankind is in danger of being destroyed—or delivered over to—demonic powers. The question already arises whether we may not be a dead end of creation. A Kabbalistic tradition maintains that at one time the animal was on a higher level than Man, but had toppled down from its heights and was delivered over to us. The history of Man is not a clockwork that runs down as if pre-ordained, it is rather a drama with an uncertain outcome and even the chance of tragedy. The final outcome hangs in the balance.

The HEAR JISRAEL (SH'MA JISRAEL) denies all absoluteness to things worldly. Belief in "absolute certainties" is idolatry, a worship of false realities. The great vision of a world with Man as its center and focus may fail. It depends on us. Will we and the world sink back into *nothingness* (the *Ayin*) or accept our true reality? Both are open possibilities. This poignant Jewish vision, though in contradiction to the visions of other peoples, again shows its relevancy.

The new Great Flood (*Mabul*) categorically calls for another courageous step of the Jews. If the "Holy People" means: "limitless rising higher," then such a historical moment has come. The key to the tormenting problems of our time is hidden on a higher level. The Torah was such a step, the beginning of the way through history, the hour for the "Founding of the People," the measure and the direction. The Torah coincided with a historical moment of extraordinary significance, the moment when historic times emerged from the abysses of pre-history, in other words, the beginning of history proper. The Torah itself is the end, the liquidation of the mythical and magical times of old. In a very concrete way it picks up where mythology leaves off. It takes a stand in relation to the facts of magic and totemism, which then were just as real as science today.

These pre-historic times were not merely the childhood of mankind, "the golden age," they were also—as related in the Torah— shot through with the demonic and pseudo-realities of a perverted life. Our life today is filled with chimeras too, with fictions and perversions, yet it may well be that the perversions of antiquity—because the nursery-time is so immensely formative—had a much greater influence. This early mankind disappeared except for a few remnants.

The saying of the Torah: "Thou shalt not make any graven image" was one of the most decisive steps taken by mankind. During the long pre-historic periods when one millennium was like the other, Man was submerged in nature and pictorial thinking. This was the embryo-time. He was the slave of nature, dominated by fear and horror, traumatic conditions reverberating to this day and the roots of our neuroses and our fear to live in the world. "Thou shalt not make any graven image" was the final knell of pre-history.

The Torah tells us that "Gan Eden," the "Garden Basis," was the original level of Man. It tells us the story of the "Founding of a People" and its concrete life through the ages, a story of plain and simple veracity. Great confrontations and controversies took place with the early historical civilizations of Chaldea and Egypt. Down through the millennia each step was always a new practical application of the Torah to ever new concrete situations. To each present time the Jewish people had a YES and NO, splitting up as it were, every new configuration, rejecting one part and accepting another, to elevate it into a higher sphere. Along with this segregation and isolation went an inner struggle leading to the elimination of what was not "pure" or "firm." Whatever was "torn" (*trefa*) was set apart from the "purified" (*kasher*). Through these two dialectically related processes of a lonely ascending and a cleansing separation the unbroken configuration of Israel emerges. Israel was integrated in the highest sense: a people of oneness. The essence of Judaism has always been unification (*Yihud*).

Where now is the answer of the Jewish people to our present time? What stand do they take in this moment of history?

How is a living Judaism possible now? There is a wrong way and a right way. The wrong way is assimilation. The right way is to renew the act of the Founding of the People, by returning to the primal origin. This primal origin is tantamount to an "ever more Here and Now," an ever greater worldly penetration and transparency. Israel's way unveils the holiness and magnificence of the world, with a more and more passionate *YES* to it. Greater worldly responsibility, greater worldly joy! We must now prepare for an act of concentration to renew the *Founding*. The obscured and almost lost true "Midst of the People" will re-emerge. "If not now, when?"

When the Jews had their encounters and controversies with nations and peoples, they played an essential role in giving rise—in each case in a dialectical step, as it were—to new movements which were accepted by others and changed them greatly from the time of the Bible to Christianity, to Islam, to modern socialism. Each time these new movements seemed to drown out the Jews, and for a moment they seemed to have come to the end of their history and to be superfluous. But each time the Jewish people, like a granite rock, re-emerged from the flood, more fortified, more concrete, because brought to a higher level by a new act of concentration and re-activated by a new realization of its essence.

Once again Judaism today seems to be drowned out. It has retreated into three narrower areas of worldly existence: science and technology, the enjoyments of life and the problems of a new socio-economic order. These are the areas where the modern Jew feels happy and so completely satisfied that he no longer needs to make room for Jewish living. Or, if such an attempt is made, the conflict with present-day life may lead to a violation of the soul, to neurotic instabilities.

Modern life gets sustenance from three sources: (1) Science and its consequences, emancipating man ever more from nature. He has been ransomed from the "house of bondage," the bondage of nature. (2) Modern sentiment: rejection of asceticism, repression and world-withdrawal. The worldly man now supersedes the old religious type. Optimism is a basic Jewish feeling, because joy is a command and this sets Judaism apart from pessimistic systems. (3) A predominant concern with social problems, which reveals the basic Jewish emphasis on justice.

But neither the merely scientific nor the worldly nor the socially-directed man is fully a Jew. These are half-truths, one-sided fragments. The unification of these parts, the key to their truth, can only be found on a higher level. Judaism is only visible from inside itself, from its own place. It is, so to speak, only an inside; its outside is merely a shell. Its great creations of science, its joy of life and its social conceptions are not yet sufficiently alive as long as they are not related to this inner reality.

If the primal Midst, necessary for the gathering-in from the confusion of today, is to re-appear, assimilation in all its meanings must be better understood. It is not worthwhile to engage in a discussion about deliberate assimilation; the main problem lies in being driven into it unintentionally, not being conscious of it at all. The Jew tries to escape from his unending task in three kinds of way, all ending in an abyss: by conceiving of Judaism as a religion, a nation or as a culture. Each of these misconceptions loads the precious treasure of Judaism onto a sinking boat. Religion, nation, culture have all become utterly suspect, and the profound doubt about them is closely connected with the immense shock mankind is afflicted with. These venerable structures are segments which by themselves can never lead to a genuine reality. They too are waiting for their redemption. Judaism is not a religion, nation or culture.

But if it is not all of that, what is it? This question is not a question because it asks for a "definition" where no "definition" can be given. Judaism can only be defined by itself and by nothing else. However great the manifestations of nature or of peoples, they cannot define the Jews; their configuration is beyond all such structures.

(1) *Religion* in the traditional sense has tended to separate the soul from the world and this is an attitude alien to Judaism whose aim is the "sanctification of our daily life." The Jew does not look for an hereafter. For him the world is not "a vale of tears," but is good and must be established in fullness. Only then will it reveal its true, paradisical character. The transformation of the world into the world-to-come, which is the world in its perfection and sanctity, is the basic vision of the Jews. "If you want to see the invisible, you must have an open eye for the visible" (*Zohar*). The Jew accepts every manifestation of concrete reality. According to the prophecies of Secharya "even the little bells of the horses, and the pots and pans will be holy." Eating, drinking, clothing, dwelling and all the rest of everyday life with its many ramifications are included in the Jewish discipline. A beautiful saying goes that "holiness lies in the innermost of the world, but nobody has yet bowed down deeply enough to lift it up." This sublime and humble attitude towards reality, this "absolute realism" differs widely from the world-weariness of other religions, which by inclination are dualistic, tearing apart truth and the world. Judaism binds them together.

Our forefathers, at the time of the emancipation of the Jews in Europe, were not inclined to be assimilated. They honestly wanted to benefit Judaism and believed it could be done by confining it to a mere confession of faith. They forgot that holiness is inseparably bound with a living people. Jewish law makes many demands on the individual, but some are directed to the whole of the people, as in the prayers that use the word "we" and not "I." Emancipation also brought many valuable things, for instance studious research into the Scriptures and the cultivation of our great treasure, the Hebrew language. Yet simultaneously it led to a dilution and formalism. The category "religion" was much too narrow, too weak and too disputed to shoulder the giant weight of Judaism.

(2) *The nation.* Any nationality is conditioned by nature. In a nation man is tied to the soil and race, and his task is to melt the elements of nature into human elements.

Because Jewishness is not "nature" and not biological, any attempt to conceive the Jewish people as a "race" must fail. Universality is a keyword of Judaism. The Exodus from Egypt, the "house of bondage," was the result of a giant challenge to embark on a universal way. The Jewish people is universal because it is focused by the highest *Yihud* (Unity), by the fact that the Absolute Reality, the *NAME*, dwells in their Midst.

Techniques and social changes today are liquidating the obsolete divisions of separate nationalities. The maelstrom whirling man around and tearing him loose from his strongholds no longer allows for outworn groupings. The world is being levelled-off, equalized. The end of nationalism is foreshadowed in a last flare-up. An awesome convulsion of mankind threatens to anihilate friend and foe alike. Such a dreadful end cannot be averted by soothing words. Nationalism must run its course and follow its own laws, which are the laws of nature, and nature is without mercy. In its realm there are no ethics, only might. Ethics is exclusively the law of mankind. Peace is attainable on the level of Judaism, whose key-word is peace (*Shalom*).

The convulsions of nationalism coincide with the mighty revolution of modern science. Physics and mathematics are uprooting the old concepts of nature. The basis of all mythical thinking and of life oriented around mythos is being destroyed. Nature, seen as the "genuine reality," is dissolving into equations.

Zionism mistakenly wants to coordinate the Jewish people with the nations and nationalism. Just as the emancipation transplanted our writings into the context of modern times, so Zionism has transplanted the land (*Erez Jisrael*) into the context of modern thought. It has renewed the focal importance of *Erez Jisrael* in the life of Judaism. But one cannot say that the revival of Judaism is the work of Zionism. This pronouncement would have to be reversed, for Zionism is the result of the revival of Judaism. The Jewish genius has chosen the conception of Zion in order to survive. Zionism is passionately and deeply resolved to overcome assimilation, as the Jews at the time of the emancipation were. Yet, in both instances assimilation has not been overcome. Nothing worthy of the name Zion can be established as a political state or by political maneuvering.

The danger for Judaism all over the world is so great that one has to anticipate an over-all attack. The true solution of the "Jewish problem" lies in the improvement of mankind's social structure. In particular the closed, separate *national* settlement cannot and will not be the future model for human communities. The general structure of mankind will undergo such essential changes that *our* way of life will become antiquated. Some factions in the Zionist movement understand this. They are right. But there is a lack of general understanding of this maximalism.

(3) Finally, *culture.* Some people hold that Judaism is merely a peculiar culture or a special spiritual or ethical attitude. This is the weakest of all the attempts to renew Judaism on a level lower than itself. It overlooks the point that culture is the end-product of a given grouping of men, but never a basis or a beginning. Every culture has within it elements which may become universal. The higher a culture the more remote it is from its origin, tending to become human possession. Ethical and spiritual attitudes have the same tendency.

The Jewish people are not an ethical society or a church. In this conception the danger is implicit of Judaism dissipating into a branch of Christianity. Already at the time of the rise of Christianity this possibility was foreseen, and one of Judaism's greatest achievements was that measures were taken to ward it off. After repudiating Christianity, in a mighty act of concentration, Judaism overcame this danger without bleeding to death. Culture does not lead to any solid ground on which to constitute Judaism anew. The idea of culture has been so undermined by the critical condition of mankind that it is itself badly in need of a renewal.

The last great historical step of the Jews was Hassidism. This was their answer to the emerging bourgeois and individualistic epoch with its cult of the soul. Traditional Judaism even today has a semblance of Hassidism. Unassimilated Judaism always adheres to some forms of past epochs. Only a small segment of "problematic" Jews stands between tradition and decay, and these "returning" ones are just those who sound the clarion call for regeneration. Why is it so difficult today to be a Jew? Certainly not because the responsibility itself is so great. That would be a rather superficial interpretation. In his innermost the Jew longs for this burden if he only knew how to actualize it! It is so difficult because the tradition is no longer carried on its original immediate vitality and fire, but is tied to tasks which no longer are actual. That he is Jewish is not what makes the modern Jew so tragically split and wavering. His fundamental opposition to the ways of other nations could enhance his life rather than stunt it.

It is a principle in Judaism that nothing is lost, once it has been within the life of the people and therefore taken up to a higher level. Remembrance of things past is the elementary vital principle of the Jewish people, a remembrance that can make the past present. To be a Jew means to remember. The entire life of the people is tied into this remembrance, out of which comes historical existence. All the tasks to which Judaism has dedicated itself are still present. This however does not mean that each of these past moments is a living actuality. Many are, or should be in the subconscious of the Jewish people, somewhat like breathing and the heartbeat in our body.

To imitate the life of only a few generations ago is the least possible. The necessity of associating Judaism with the problems and actualities of each period of history always has to be coupled with a new step. Part of the preparation for the Jewish gathering-in is scrutinizing the problems and changes in the realm of intellect and science, modes of living, of social structures, and rejecting or integrating them into the Jewish way of life.

"The Torah does not speak in the language of the angels." It speaks in the language of concrete, living man. It started the Jew on his way through history, through all the religions, through the wildest storms, blunders and perversities. It is written with the blood of countless martyrs. It is an unending discussion of Jew with Jew. Boundless treasures of wisdom, experience and sanctified events are contained in it. The Talmud is a record of discourses through centuries, in which the details of actual everyday life are scrutinized "in the face of the Absolute." This gigantic protocol was further supplemented by commentaries. In a different way the Kabbalists continued the never-ending discussion. Is it now to become silent in this time of chaos and confusion?

Mankind in general seems to disintegrate into atoms. But the Jewish world means the united world with the Unity (*Yihud*) as the foundation. The earmark of activities called "black magic" is the inability to achieve unification. Isolated fragments then strive to control the human center, using it for their own limited and destructive purposes. One should however not discount the possibility that this process of disintegration may be due to a weakness of the center. In that case the individual might have to choose isolation, not out of selfishness, but with sincere sorrow. A humble waiting may help to restore the lost center. Hope lies in the fact that destructive powers again and again have failed, because they are unable to create unity among themselves. Israel, as the realm of unity and wholeness, that is *Peace (Shalom)*, cannot contain within it this sickness of the world. The true goal of Judaism is not power; rather power should come to an end in it once and for all.

The next historical step of the Jews is to obey again the Biblical command to Abraham: *"Go away, thou"* (*"Lekh lekha"*), away from the confusions of today onto a higher madriga. And this should be the paradigm, instead of the rules and orders of the nations shaken by the fevers of decay. The principles of the religions, nationalities, races, cultures and politics are in need of help, but are unable to give help. It is high time for a return to the original structure of Judaism, if a debacle is not to overcome the Jews.

The miraculous story of the Jews, their strong hold on life, their fathomless memory and adherence to absolute orders, this marvel rests on the unification in the absolute *Yihud*. Their strength and dynamic lie in the innermost recesses and not outside as with most other groupings. Most other groupings derive their unity either from nature or from forces outside or above themselves. Between pre-or-dained compulsions life then runs its course, shorter or longer, mod-estly or magnificently. But the Founded People has all its powers stored up in its innermost, except one—THE NAME. We can only say HE is in our Midst (*bekirbenu*).

The Jewish people live between two poles or borders, language and body. It is one of the greatest insights of Judaism that language, the word, is the root of all things. Creation, *genuine creation out-of-nothing* (*yesh me ayin*), originates in the Word. "HE spoke." Even light, the basic principle of modern physics, emanates from the Word. Whatever we encounter, innermost or outermost, is "crea-ture." That means: nothing in itself has reality; it was "spoken" and given its reality in its own place.

The creative power of language is decaying today. It is the highest phenomenon, the maximal. The Hebrew language is the language of languages. To convert it into a "means of communication" is a misconception. It demands that "we do not take the words into our mouth; we must enter into the words like entering into a sanctuary." The renascence of Judaism greatly depends on a genuine revival of the Hebrew language on a higher level.

Although language serves and even creates communication it is more than that. Because of its absoluteness it makes for openness, the real essence of man. Openness is the innermost character of Judaism. The way downward is blocked. Language is the transcendence of life over itself.

The other pole of the people is the body. Reality can only be achieved with body, its inherent hunger and thirst, its vulnerability, its lust and its anxiety. Out of its inexorable earnestness, out of its afflictions and the ever-present danger of death, the body gives rise to enormous configurations, ascending higher until they become language. The guarantee of right action lies in a right physicality. The mere *wish* to act rightly does not get us very far. The Ritual creates a body from which the right action can flow in fulness.

Language borders the Absolute, while the body is totally relative and conditioned, the epitome of conditionality. The body should be, nevertheless, extraordinarily pure, solid and strong, the only kind of a body which can become permeable to the highest light. As modern physics has shown there is nothing absolute in nature, nature is relative through and through. There are only "fields," constantly changing relations without any fixed points. The "field-theoretical" explanation shows that all physical manifestations are nothing but a web of space and time. If there can no longer be an absolute body, if there are only relative bodies, then body as the private property of the soul has been overcome, and the collective body is on the way to being established. The collectivity of language is guaranteed by its absoluteness and the collectivity of body by its relativity.

Relative body and absolute language are the two poles of the people. Language that became body and body redeemed in the word. But these two poles and the life of the people flowing between them like an electric current are not outside of the people. No external worlds of ideas, primal images, gods, fates or powers reign over the

Jews. Through language this world is in the innermost of the people. The body is dependent on the people, the people is not dependent on what we call corporeality. Language and body both are capable of establishing a community either alone or together. Language is collective, but body is too. The awareness that Judaism has not only a collective language but also a collective body is of utmost importance. Therein the ever-lasting memory of the Jews is embedded, subconsciously, as it is consciously in language. In the Ritual the Absolute NAME is subconsciously present, like the breath of a healthy organism. Therefore genuine religiosity does not have to utter the NAME.

As body develops, culture and "cult" result. Finally the Word emerges. When the Word descends, it goes the way of the Ritual, ending in the body. In this way cult flows into language and Ritual into body. The meaning of the Ritual is to create body, but pure body, free of impurity. Since the Ritual is in decay the Jewish revival is impeded. Without Ritual a new configuration of the people cannot take place. Why is it that ever more Jews cannot accept the Ritual? Is it because of weakness or inertia? This would be too easy an explanation. We have no right to doubt the willingness of many a Jew to take gladly upon himself the burdensome task of the Ritual. But quite a few feel frustrated rather than elevated by the Ritual. Yet how can there be a Jewish people without a strict Ritual? What other kind of principle would be strong enough to unite the Jews? What could suffice to give them enough strength to withstand the tempting voices of a seemingly more emancipated world? How could an assemblage be accomplished without any order of daily life, or order of the body with its rhythms, nourishments and multitudes of forms and shapes?

Ritual and cult are two streams (like the streams of blood in our veins and arteries), which regulate the metabolism of the people and make an ever-lasting interplay between the Word and the body. The Word addresses the higher spheres and gets an answer. The body closes up, condenses and concretizes. This metabolism is now disrupted. No Word ascends from the depth of the body, and no Word descends to condense and focus the body. Thus the people is without the Word and without the body. A broken-down metabolism is wearily circling around a tepid middle-course, where body without shape, and Word without truth meet in idle talk. Relinquishing the Ritual and its counter-part, the cult, has impaired the healthy circulation. The impossibility of keeping any Ritual is perhaps the fundamental reason for the deterioration of mankind. Ritual means the order in accordance with which a people has been founded. It means the concrete structure of that people and above all its characteristic physiognomy. Ritual is the order of life of a people. A founded people, however, must again and again renew the original act that brought it into being, and the Ritual is this recurring renewal.

The never-interrupted rebirth that gave new strength to the body of a people is not possible without a dialectical counterplay. A two-fold aspect is always involved. Lifting-out-from, and rising-higher-into means the simultaneous letting-go-of and keeping-apart-from. With an outward segregation necessarily goes an inner discarding. The body of the people discards elements that have come from the outside, but have been lived with for a long time and have become part of it. Every important turning-point in history bears the marks of such a separation. What does "discarding" mean? If one can "name" something, one can "know" it; and what is "known" loses its power over us. The "known" and the "defined" becomes a thing and is at our mercy. Judaism by "naming" the powers attempts to render them powerless. Such "discarding" has weakened the gods and the false realities. When the world is redeemed from the primal split—separation of the "tree of knowledge" from the "tree of life" —then the Full NAME will appear over the full world and the original Unity (*Yihud*) be restored.

There is a three-fold principle of negation to be repudiated: murder, idolatry, incest. *Murder* means to deprive a person of his place in the world. Everybody and even everything has a legitimate place. The genuine places do not war against each other. Evil ensues only when man tries to displace his fellow-man. We should be mindful of the saying: "To make someone publicly ashamed so that the blood rushes to his face, is almost equivalent to spilling his blood."

Each step of the Jews in the course of history was an application of the basic Jewish principle: to abolish *idolatry*. Thus it could be said that "he who is free of idolatry is called a Jew." The world is full of evil principles, of subtle pseudo-realities and almost imperceptibly fine poisons much more destructive than gross idols. These evils infiltrate even into the highest spiritual spheres. Opposition to idolatry is the hallmark of the purity of Judaism. In ancient times the Ritual discarded the powerful, perverted pre-world of mythology and magic. In later times the "mind" was the object of the Ritual's concern. Mind is by no means the ultimate reality for the Jewish conception of the world. It will have to be dethroned, but not in favor of the equally unreal principle of merely biological life, a most dangerous deception of our time.

Incest, in its profoundest meaning, does not refer to sexual perversities only. Egotism, incapable of going beyond itself, is already incest. Upon these far-reaching insights the Ritual has been constituted. Its formative powers for daily renewal are based upon the severe demands implicit in it.

When the Ritual is falling short of its task to build a people's body, it merely remains an oppressive fetter. When it no longer repeats and renews the founding act of the people, it becomes a kind of manacling, leading to an emaciation, perhaps even to insincerity, self-delusion and the wish to escape, to evade. When the Biblical Ritual does not gather together the people in the highest *Yihud*, united under the Absolute NAME, then rejection of or indifference to the Ritual is the result.

A people cannot last long without a Ritual because it cannot be without a body. A collective without a collective body is relatively short-lived. A collective that has both body and Word in its innermost is absolute and imperishable, true and mighty. Therefore the question arises: what is the idolatry of today and the incest of today? What is it that we should lock up and seal with the power of the Ritual? What is it that is being discarded today? It looks as if vast spheres of our existence are being left behind at this terrible moment of history.

Mighty structures of our existence threatening to overpower mankind are now being called by their "names" and are slipping below the human level. As never before we are close to understanding what nature is, and to call it by its true "name." Nature, when seen as a myth vanishes. The gods, the idols are dying. In our subconscious vast layers of emotions are coming to light, and an entire underworld of horror is being exposed. A legion of fiends, our fears and superstitious adorations, are being unmasked and will have to surrender to the sovereignty of humanity. Above all, the economic process will have to be brought to submission and discarded. Economy, which embraces the immediate needs of man, is the place of the most embittered fights at present. It is, so to speak, the key-position from which modern problems can be outgrown. The economic process, devastating mankind like a cosmic blight, will be brought under human control.

In these discardings the Jews have a leading role, as in the case of Einstein, Freud, Marx and others. The key to the problems of a given level always lies on the next higher level, whether with regard to the mastery of the powers, or downgrading them to a level below the level of man, deeper realities become apparent. From the higher planes we arrive at levels more primal than nature, more soulful than soul, more concrete than economy.

Never has the Jewish people been weakened by the giant process of discarding. Each time its own essence has been brought more clearly into view. Man is still infantile when it comes to facing the world; he does not know yet how to handle it. He wants to escape like a frightened child and take refuge in fairy tales, or ruin the world as a child ruins its toys. We are just beginning to understand and get acquainted with life in this world, but we remain in a state of dependency, hesitation and regression, and do not dare to walk onward. The Jew, strengthened by his confidence and optimism, will be in the frontline of those who can move on again. He knows that the "full" world is good and that the sickness of man is but a lack of courage to enter into it.

So exalted a task necessitates the awakening of the People. But the new concentration, the attainment of the new madriga, the renewal of the primordial, requires a new Midst. The Ritual must become manifest as what it has been from primordial times, namely the miraculous possibility of beginning ever anew. It is a way of life in whose center the Absolute Reality dwells, a way which enables man to co-exist with the incandescence of the NAME and not be consumed by it. Some preparatory steps are necessary. We need the help of those who clearly recognize the problems of our time, the relationship of the Jewish people to the world at large, the nations and their achievements. They must be those who still have a thorough knowledge of the tradition, as well as those who have a knowledge of the most advanced science of today. They need to be in close touch with the whole people, because the Midst can only be established by the Whole of the People. The aim is that supreme event, when the never-ending discourse of the Jews finds its Midst, an ever-lasting assembly of this Whole of the People.

Job *

Mankind is overwhelmed to-day by a crisis unequalled in history. Everyone speaks of the crisis, but few realize its profundity. Many think it is only a disturbance which will 'blow over.' Few realize that the basis of human existence is in question; that the roots of human existence are being exposed. And the question of questions emerges: whether man is, perhaps, a kind of blind alley of nature, into which the cosmos has run. Is man, perhaps, a kind of natural monster, destined to die out?

At this moment of profound crisis a new possibility arises for man, which may be made clear by the struggle between what is called the 'superstructure' and the 'substructure' of human life. Our religions, our philosophies, ideals and social institutions are built upon a so-called 'substructure.' A tremendous realm of subconscious life lies beneath us, of unknown duration through prehistoric time. We are only just beginning to discover this subconscious life of the soul, as we are only just beginning to examine the economic basis of our culture. And we are now making the overpowering discovery that our cultural life, our ideals, our art and our justice are essentially a 'superstructure' upon this 'substructure,' an expression of the unconscious underworld of our being. This ideology of our shining world of culture roots in this subconscious life. Psychoanalysis,

* The quotation marks and capital letters used in the original printing (*Purpose*, Vol. 9, No. 3, July-Sept. 1937) have been retained in this printing.

Marxist analysis, biology and anthropology have unveiled the base of the superstructure. Nothing remains which we do not need to question. It has often happened before in history that some things were in question. But it has never happened before that everything, without exception, was in question.

But we are of necessity investigating this world of the subconscious by means of our consciousness of to-day, our modern culture and science. The 'superstructure' itself reveals the 'substructure.' And this 'substructure' appears as a world of illusions, of fantasies, of superstitions; a prehistory, filled with terrors, destroying man's confidence in life itself. These prehistoric times, which we must regard as our racial 'nursery,' are filled with fear. Out of this fear, and of these illusions, there arose deep perversions, which have injured the human soul. Economic analysis shows a world of social disorder and injustice—a chaos, over which the showy edifices of culture have been erected. Thus, if on the one hand our penetration into the 'substructure' unveils the 'superstructure,' on the other hand, the 'superstructure' unveils the 'substructure.' The one world negates the other! These two worlds dissolve, reciprocally. And this dissolution goes so far that even Nature dissolves in the struggle between these two realms. Modern physics dissolves Nature in a system of cold mathematical equations.

Can we gain some standpoint, outside of the chaotic dissolution? If a procession passes through a city I must take up a position at a place where the procession will pass. Even the most beautiful place will not avail me if the procession does not pass that way.

A standpoint of this sort, which will give us an outlook upon greater realities, is the Book Of Job, in the Bible. A standpoint of great antiquity and yet still quite incomprehensively new. One of the mightiest attempts to break through to a greater and higher reality. The Book Of Job is a masterly composition in majestic language, a poetic utterance of a beauty which has inspired the greatest poets of the world. The poem is traditionally ascribed to the time of Moses.

The Book Of Job is one of the most difficult writings ever written, because of the extraordinary height of the viewpoint found in it. On the other hand, the description of events in it is very easy to understand. It is the story of a man who was a thoroughly upright, righteous man, of deep piety, filled with faith in God; good and just towards his fellow-men. This man was exceptionally blessed with goods and with children. And then one day, Satan (the devil) appeared before God and said to God: "This man is thy servant only as long as he is blessed with the abundance of good fortune. But give him into my hand, and he will renounce thee to thy face." Whereupon God, in order to try Job and Satan, gave this upright man into the hands of Satan. "All that he has is in thy power, only upon himself put not forth thy hand." And now misfortune falls upon Job. Enemies force their way into his house. They burn his goods. And they murder his children. But Job does not waver in his faith in God. He humbly accepts his fate. Whereupon Satan again appears before God and demands: "Let me touch him, himself. And thou wilt see, he will renounce thee to thy face." And God gives Job himself into the hands of Satan. "Behold, he is in thy hand; only spare his life." And now Job is smitten with disease and leprosy. But he still remains unshaken in his faith. Three friends come to him and try to console him. In his conversation with them Job finally yields. He curses the day he was born. He asks why this fate has struck him. And the more his friends try to console him, the more passionately does Job rage. Why must the upright suffer? And why does the blasphemer succeed? Where is divine justice? His friends try to answer his questions and his doubt. "No one may say that he is upright." In statement and counterstatement, this conversation rises to dramatic heights. Job becomes ever more terribly enraged. And his friends retort ever more passionately that he is a sinner, who will not see that he is suffering a deserved punishment. His suffering, they say, is a punishment for his sinfulness. In mighty words Job repudiates this consolation as untrue. It does nothing to overcome his doubt in divine justice.

The names of Job's friends give the first clue to the meaning of the story. Eliphas, Bildad and Zophar are the names of underworld figures. Eliphas—the 'gold-god, Pluto.' Bildad—the 'destroyer.' Zophar—the 'god of the dead.' These three are, if we were to explain them in the language of modern psychoanalysis, voices of one's own subconscious impulses which have become visible and audible—a kind of self-reproach. These names are symbolic, as are the names of the three daughters of Job. Jemima—the life preservation instinct.

Kezia—that which shortens life, that which Freud would call the death instinct, the deep instinct to refuse to live in the world. That is the antithesis to Jemima, who represents the life instinct. And the third—Keren Ha Puch, 'the horn of change,' the Cornucopia, the abundance in which the great Yes and No fuse into one. The name Job itself means: the tested one.

The greatness of the Book Of Job consists first in the fact that it disclaims these three friends as demoniacal underworld figures. At the end of the book the wrath of God breaks out against the three consolers, because they did not talk 'uprightly.' Their consolation is no consolation. It is false, and those who utter it have shown Job no love. There are situations in which consolations are cruel and unseemly. "Where a corpse lies, one does not utter consolations." One can help. But one can not console with words.

But what is the right answer to Job's problem? A new figure appears. Elihu. The literal translation of this name is: My God is he. He is different from the three friends, for he does not attack Job. To be sure, he does not deny that no one may think himself upright. But he does not say that Job is suffering a punishment. He only asks that Job adjust himself to his suffering, for everything originates in God. He offers no explanation. The cause of Job's suffering is a mystery. This answer, too, is insufficient but it forms the transition to the answer which God himself gives to Job. God answers Job in a storm.

The answer of God is so strange, and appears to have so little connection with Job's tragedy and with his anguished questions, that mountains of difficulties pile up before our comprehension. God's answer is apparently so entirely without relation to Job's question that foolish critics have believed this part of the book to be a later addition, originating from another source. In this misunderstanding we see how difficult it is to comprehend the basic idea of the Book Of Job. God says to Job: "Gird up now thy loins like a man." He calls to his bravery and power. And God continues: "For I will demand of thee . . ." And now there follow, in majestic speech, questions all of which refer to nature, to the animal world, the life of the earth and the atmosphere, the cosmos. And God asks again and again: "Where wast thou when I laid the foundations of the earth? Who determined the measures thereof? Who stretched the line upon it?

Where wast thou when the morning stars sang together? Where wast thou when I played with the leviathan?" (The leviathan, the mythical monster of the primitive world which devoured everything.) "Where wast thou when I bound the Pleiades and Orion?" And again and again God repeats His question: "What doest thou know of my governance of nature?" "Where wast thou when I created all this?" What is most characteristic of this 'answer' of God is that it is really no answer at all. Job sought to establish God's justice, and God answers with cosmology. In a very deep sense this answer might be called ironic. Job receives no answer at all. How can this riddle be understood?

In the Book Of Job we are dealing with a so-called 'theodicy,' that is, an attempt to justify God, in the face of the evil in the world. Where is God's justice if the blasphemer triumph and the upright suffer? The 'answer' of the Book Of Job reaches heights unscaled by any other solution of the world mystery. This old Hebraic theodicy rejects all theodicy. God does not excuse himself! God is the absolute standard. We may not take the events in the world as starting points, and then invent a concept of God which can be brought into harmony with the contradictions and injustices of the world. There is only one standard for God's justice. And it lies in God Himself. There is no standard with which God can be measured. That which we call God *is* the standard, and human wisdom consists in bringing events in the world into harmony with this standard.

The 'answer' of the Book Of Job is that we have not yet rightly understood. We have viewed the world with our human eyes, judging God according to human standards. We have not, as we should have done, judged human standards by God's order of the universe. To accept this absolute standard would give the world the highest of all chances to rise again and again above the level of human judgment!

A very modern reference—the achievement and attitude of Einstein—will perhaps make this clearer. How was the Relativity theory discovered? The nature of light and its motion were investigated, and *space* was taken as a standard. Firm, spatial standards were imposed on the nature of light to measure it. One day, the physicist

Michelson was conducting an experiment in which certain changes in the form and motion of light were to be expected. But these changes did not occur. Thinking of similar facts, Einstein had a brilliant intuition: "Why not," he said, "reverse the relation we have assumed between light and space, and base our measurements on the assumption that light, not space, is the invariable? Perhaps, we should not measure light with spatial standards; the variable factor is perhaps space, and not light." This, in a few words, is the germ of the relativity theory. Here the position of the observer was completely reversed.

Infinitely more powerful is the reversal in the Book Of Job. Here God is no longer measured by the world, by the order or disorder of the world. But the world is measured by God. The standard is here God. And that which changes is the world. The Book Of Job leads us to a deeper understanding of the world.

What we have not rightly understood is disclosed in Job's problem and the answers of the three friends which the Book Of Job condemns so strongly. Suffering is not only a 'punishment.' If it were a punishment, then, to be sure, incalculable numbers of the innocent would be affected. The most widespread suffering is poverty. Yet we cannot imagine that the poor have a monopoly of guilt.

To be sure, there is another doctrine, the Indian doctrine of reincarnation. It explains suffering on the basis of our actions in earlier existences on earth. And the good and evil which we did in these lives pile up in an account of debit and credit. The so-called 'Karma.' What we have sown in these earlier lives we now reap in the present life. This interpretation is essentially the same as that of the three friends of Job. We ourselves are to blame for our suffering. This interpretation, that everybody's suffering is explained by *his own sins,* is sharply rejected in the Book Of Job.

The interpretation of human life according to reward and punishment, achievement and remuneration, is a lower one. There is a lovely tale of a famous Rabbi. Once, for the first time in his life, he let out a deep sigh. Whereupon a voice resounded from heaven which said: "Thou hast now lost thy share in the coming time of the Messiah." For in this sigh, he had forgotten that everything which hap-

pens, no matter what, is good, because it comes from God. Whereupon he answered this voice: "That's splendid. For now I can do the
right without thinking of being rewarded."

Man's true life has nothing to do with weighing upon a scale—
with a balancing of deed and remuneration. Man's honor and dignity are not affected by the fate which he suffers. The God Who is
spoken of here is not a God of fate. He reveals nothing as to why
one suffers this fate and another suffers a different fate. This God is
associated with the roots of the human being, but not with man's
fate. God's justice would be questioned if man's essence should be
affected. God says that Job is right. Job is justified in his revolt against
the sphere of fate. And the answers and consolations of his friends
are false. Or, as it is called in God's answer, 'not upright.' The true
answer is not that Job is suffering a punishment. This answer is much
too flat. The vision must be raised higher before we can gain the complete view.

The sufferer is thus not a reprobate. Another thing in which the
three friends were wrong is that they reproach the *other* with wickedness. One can rightly recognize no wickedness more deeply than one's
own. One can very well talk of the baseness of one's self, but not of
the baseness of the other. It is not true that in suffering each of us
must answer only for himself. Everyone must answer for the other.
Suffering has very little to do with individual fate, it belongs to a
much higher sphere than mere fate. Fate is what each of us experiences of fortune and misfortune. But man in truth inhabits a powerful sphere, in which the realm of fate sinks immeasurably beneath
us. Suffering in the world stands for responsibility. Some wear the
responsibility well; they carry the burden and suffer under it. These
are the strongest, they suffer vicariously for others. Job carried a responsibility for the demonic sphere of fate. The weak are often too
weak to suffer. Those whom we call wicked and transgressors are often
without insight and without strength. Their vitality breaks under the
strain of suffering; they are infantile. There is a deep vision in the
theory of the anthropologist Lombroso, who taught: The criminal
is a type which is physically conditioned—in fact, an 'atavistic type,'
a rebound to primitive levels. The wicked are too dull to be able to

carry the deep problematique which constitutes the mystery of the world.

Suffering is not the payment of a debt, but rather a burden of responsibility. Job did not have to answer for sins which he had committed. He took upon himself the terrible problem of suffering. The question with which he wrestled is a basic question of the order of the world, the struggle between God and Satan. Or, if we should express this, not in the old religious words, but in our modern language, it is the question of whether the world is meaningful or meaningless. Is the world good or evil? Is it worthless to live in the world and futile? And ought we to flee it? These contradictions struggle within us.

In a splendid small pamphlet (*Beyond the Pleasure Principle*) Freud shows that the human psyche is not determined only by the sexual (erotic) instinct as he originally believed. He finds another instinct in the human psyche, the death instinct. The psyche desires but fears life. Jemima and Kezia: the urge for life and the tendency to flee the world, are in conflict in the human soul. And resolution of the conflict may not yet be in sight.

At the end of the Book Of Job everything is returned to Job: his wealth, his health, and his children also. Job does not perish like the Greek heroes. An abyss lies between them, the Hebrew and the Greek viewpoint, into which we cannot now enter.

But let us ask with Job: What does the blind Realm of Fate stand for? What kind of strange sphere is this, in which God leaves everything to the operation of chance? We have already observed that God's answer to Job does not appear to meet the cry of his soul. God speaks of the cosmos. "Where wast thou, man," asks God, "when I founded the cosmos?" God answered cosmologically in order to reveal to Job Job's own secret thoughts. This whole question of justification belongs to a lower sphere. In the cosmos, to be sure, everything takes place according to law. There everything is weighed against everything else. One force corresponds exactly to another; all is balanced. There cause and effect rule. Nature is the realm of Fate. Job, with his doubt, has not penetrated more deeply than to the question: What is the cause of my suffering? He takes God as a kind of cause, a natural force. God is to him a part of the universe; perhaps the top or the apex of the universe; or the basis of the universe. But God is entirely bound up in this game of cause and effect, in this great mechanism of the cosmos. Thus, this God of Job's is a cosmological God. It is a God who is supposed to explain the phenomena of nature.

But God is not only a principle whereby the universe can be explained or given meaning. That is the God of the Theologians—an abstract God. And this concept of God is what we today consider obsolete. If we wish to describe natural phenomena, we now do it scientifically. And it seems superstitious to us to ascribe a kind of director to all this great activity of the cosmos.

Thus, we are led forward to the concept of God proclaimed by the Book Of Job, which does not conflict with the most enlightened ideas in modern intellectual development. And these modern ideas are in essence the same that have everywhere illuminated the highest reaches of the human mind. It is so strange in our times that ideas which lie only a short distance behind us in time are already obsolete and covered with dust. And age-old ideas are gaining extraordinary timeliness. And indeed, the more timely, the more they refer to the elementary bases of human nature, and return to the starting point of human evolution. The more they have these characteristics, the more they inspire us with the necessary hope to begin once more all over again from the very beginning.

Job's question was a cosmological question. And God answers it cosmologically, not, as our erroneous assumption would require, as though everything in the cosmos should come out right, as in a calculation. But as an eagle flies over the abyss which lies beneath him, so does the Book of Job fly over the cosmos. God is not only a natural force, were it even the highest. And man, too, is not only a piece of nature. And the relation between man and God is not only a settlement which must balance like an account. Could you even admit such a bank-account basis in a deep relationship between two friends? God did not touch the being of Job at all, only his fate. But man's fate is not the man. The cosmos is a world of fate. But the relation between God and man is ethical. It is based on freedom and on dignity. Job's essential dignity has not been wounded at all.

On the contrary, he is honoured in having to uncover the basic problem of the world: the role of the negative and the destructive in the world.

In the language of the old religions, Satan—the name comes from the word 'to bend'—bends back the upward evolution of the world. 'Wicked' are all those tendencies which place man's life in fantasies of 'another world' or keep him on the childhood level of mankind—the danger which psychoanalysis characterises as 'infantilism'. Job has not been treated any more unjustly than, let us say, the captain of a ship, who is killed in a shipwreck, because his honour demands of him that he remain to the end on the ship.

That is why God asks Job: "Wilt thou even annul my judgment? Wilt thou condemn me that thou mayest be justified?" It is not God who must be justified. And man must not be accused, as the friends of Job do. Certainly, man is not perfect. His imperfection lies in the fact that he considers himself but a piece of nature. But man is not only nature. The essence of man is that he can achieve relationship with God. Man hears the call, and he can respond. Even England's great thinker of the Renaissance, Lord Bacon, who so greatly glorified science and who founded empirical philosophy, says: "They that deny a God, destroy man's nobility, for certainly man is of kin to the beasts by his body; and if he is not of kin to God by his spirit, he is a base and ignoble creature."

In the cosmos, man and God can never come together. The pantheistic idea that God is to be found everywhere in nature, is one of the causes for the decline of the concept of God. To express it in modern language, everything is relative. Einstein's cosmos is the same as the cosmos of the Book Of Job. Nothing has reality of itself. Nature is relative through and through. Every phenomenon is itself part of an indescribably complicated net of relations. Reality is not to be found there. The Jewish tradition teaches that Abraham sought God in the cosmos. But he did not find him there. And because he could not find him there, he was driven to search for God where He reveals himself, namely in the direct conversation between God and man.

One must always so conduct one's self as if there were no God at all! We may not explain the riddle of nature by God: that would be the end of science. We may not wait for succour from God: that would be the end of human initiative. The less we concern ourselves with the idea of God in our explanation of the world and in our practical life, the more clearly will God appear. This is what the Book Of Job teaches when God asks: "Where wast thou when I founded the cosmos?" And even: "Where art thou, when I direct the cosmos?"

The more 'worldly' we live, the more powerfully we develop the world, the more clearly will the highest possibilities in the world emerge. The more we turn from the world and cast our glance toward God, the more we attempt to form a concept of God, the more will God vanish into a mere abstraction, into obsolete superstition. The Book Of Job is one of the earliest and most powerful awakenings to a realistic conception of God. Nature is but a preliminary stage; it is not the human world. The Book Of Job challenges man to enter the human world, to raise himself above Nature. This is the greatest emancipation of the human being possible. This age-old Book raises the question which is cardinal today. Is man an inessential by-product of infinite Nature, or is man the focus of the universe? Is Nature the standard by which to measure Nature? God belongs only to a completely developed world. And the completely developed world is the cosmos of love, of social justice. In Nature there is neither love nor ethical laws. Nature is determined by pitiless struggle and by death. The vision of the Book Of Job penetrates all superstition, and reaches the level expressed by the Rabbi who answered his own question, "What is God?" by saying, "I do not know. I know only one thing: He is clearly present, and beside Him nothing else is clearly present."

Articles from The Jewish Press (1955-1956)

THE DANGER FOR THE STATE OF ISRAEL
AND THE TWO ZIONISMS

It is said: "You will be called by your name, you will be seated in your place, you will be given what is yours." "No kingdom will touch its neighbors by so much as a hair's breadth." (*Yoma* and *Berachoth*.) How can such vistas be applied to the dangerous situation that has developed in the Near East? *There are two aspects of Zionism.* The one is the very truth. The other is a fallacy. In declaring that the Jews were not a "religious denomination" but a People, Zionism was absolutely right. It was a glorious deed to re-establish the *People*, which had been founded *for* the Torah and had been *focused by* the Torah. It was however fallacious to conceive the Jewish people as a "political" unity. In this misconception a great insight was again lost and, up to this very moment, all the perplexities are a consequence of the initial mistake. As a political factor Israel always has been a mere pawn in the hands of the Empires and their satellites. As a theophoric people, Israel was invincible; it survived all the great Powers. None of the momentous steps which Israel had taken in history was the result of political ambitions. All these great steps, overtaking one civilization after the other, belong to a higher order. Trust in political cunning always has ended in disappointment for the Jews, even in disaster. To say it in the words of the outcry: *"Mi iti? Mi?"* ("Who is for me? Who?" [Kings 2. 19,32]). The answer is clear—nobody! Irrevocably Israel was extricated from "normalcy," but this overtaking of the illusion of normalcy is a hope for Jew and Gentile alike.

Does all this mean the Jews should become "idealists," in the vain hope "that the just cause will triumph?" In our present situation would not such a hope be childish and unrealistic? Should the Jews rely on "miracles"? What after all are "miracles"? They are not—as the common definition has it—a breaking-up of the *natural* order of things. There are no exceptions from the laws of nature. "Miracle," in the Jewish conception means that this "natural" order, in its uninterrupted continuity, is embedded in a higher order. It is—as it were—*enveloped* by a superior order that *interprets* the *meaning* of the concatenation of events. In Jewish thought, therefore, one finds the ever-recurring belief that righteous action here below attracts the higher influence from above, thus imposing its superior order on the lower. The tragical thing in our present-day practicalism is our unawareness of the higher dimensions of the world, of anything beyond mere "practicality." That what goes beyond "management" is looked at as "moonshine." *However, the entire history of the Jews is one mighty manifestation of the "impossible."* It was only the "impossible" that succeeded; and the "possible" mostly failed.

It was said, had the Jewish people just for once lived up to keeping a *perfect* Sabbath *unanimously,* it would make an indelible impact on the world. A superior action has an almost miraculous effect on the minds of the peoples. Ultimately men are guided by mental rather than by political powers. It was an amazing insight of Freud's when he pointed out how naive it was to think that the two World Wars had been instigated by a few politicians over and against the will of the masses. What is it that actually binds millions to the rulership of small minorities? Freud says: had the masses subconsciously not agreed to wage these wars, we never would have had these wars. On the other hand it is also true that very determined spiritual and moral manifestations of the peoples can make them almost invulnerable. We know that the human spirit ultimately bows to a mighty truth. And we also know to what an extraordinary degree the Jews are capable of emanating such truth. How futile it is to meet an *overwhelming* political and economic power with a *tiny* power of the same kind! All that can be done—politically—is rather *negative*: to wriggle out with all available intelligence from the mad scramble. Nothing can be done "politically" in a positive way.

The "miracle"—the effect of the superior order of the world—so familiar to Jewish history remains a "dream" only as long as we *believe* it is a dream. We have to learn again what we have forgotten, namely, the "suddenness" of deep change. Consider the sudden climax in the Purim Story; or take the *leap* of a whole people from unspeakable depravity under the Pharaoh's yoke into the heights of humanity, achieved in one moment. Israel's way is not co-ordinatable with any political way. The admirable accomplishments at the holy ground of Erez Israel have been done by impractical dreamers. *They could achieve the impossible* because they had been—Zionists. When they try to turn politicians they may lose even the possible.

Are We Entering the Pre-Messianic Era?

It is said the Messianic Time will bring no other change—but PEACE. However, what deeper change is feasible? This is a conception of the Messiah, which is a *political* and *social* vision, and probably a very primal one. In many important sayings it is emphasized that the Messiah is a Man and not a mystical creature, and that God only is the redeemer. Jews, in whom the Messianic fire still is burning, are and always were ready to expect the coming of the Messiah the very next hour, they were prepared just as well to wait for him another thousand years. All such sayings mean to say that "we cannot force the end." The day of the Messiah (*Yemot ha Mashiah*) will not come but by the fulfillment of history—not by its annulment. There is no short circuit of the process of history. There is no anticipating the Messianic Time. Such anticipating merely opens up a side-exit for our escape from history and prevents us from going through history, there to meet the challenge put before Man. This attempt at breaking up the course of history by a mystical event presents one of the profoundest issues where the Jewish and the Christian view differ fundamentally. It is, also today, one of the controversial issues of the "Religious Crisis"—the question whether a real change can come inside of history or only beyond it. (In "theological terms"—History or Eschatology?) This question does not exist for the Jews.

The discovery of the *Dead Sea Scrolls* became a spectacular event of far greater significance than a mere archeological affair, because the Scrolls are concerned with Messianic Problems. It is the kinship that exists between our time and the time when the Scrolls were written which makes the discovery so exciting. Both eras are "end-eras." Yet there is a difference in which way these two eras look at the end. The era before the destruction of the Second Temple was inspired by an apocalyptic spirit. There was a common, general readiness to prepare for the end. Our era lacks the readiness to face the magnitude of this moment. The spirit of that ancient time, which was not unknown to us (but has now been amended and affirmed by the Scrolls), was full of Messianic expectations. "The Dead Sea Sect"—doubtless the Essenes, who had hidden the Scrolls in the caves of the Dead Sea desert—were determinedly devoted to a *Purity Ritual.* Their belief, however, was that purity can be attained *only by being detached from the people.* They had decided that a cloisterly separation, a monastic life, was the unalterable pre-requisite to accomplish this goal. Here we are at the cradle of those trends, which want to replace the people by a church. Such an abolition of the actual building up and perfecting of a concrete people *must* eventually end in the *surrogate of a mystical perfection,* and lead to the belief that the time was ripe for the Messiah to come. Here the ways of the Jews and the branching-off sects definitely part.

The Messianic vistas distinguish between the Suffering Messiah and the Triumphant Messiah. The Suffering Messiah, as he appears in the Prophet Isaiah (Chap. 53) "is despised and rejected by all and vicariously carries the sins of all of us." Not a single individual, the Suffering Messiah is Israel—the People. The Suffering Messiah is always with us, but the Triumphant Messiah—though he is waiting in all the generations—is concealed until the fulfillment is brought about. Proclaiming the Messianic end inside of the unmitigated corruption is a contradiction in terms. The Scrolls tell us of a Jewish inside-story, a new, slowly developing Messianic pattern, which was always well known to Jewish historians, and of which the Gospels are only a late and last sediment. It was rightly stated that the Founder of Christianity was the first self-proclaimed Messiah. The end of all Messianic Self-Proclamation occurred in the catastrophe of Sabbatai Zwi. He who proclaims to be the Messiah cannot be the Messiah. The Triumphant Messiah is still waiting, but he is waiting—for us.

WHY DO THE NATIONS RAGE?

It is said, hosts of angels had to be eliminated because of their opposition to the creation of Man. Thus the way was opened for Man to supersede and suspend many stages and regions beneath himself. There is a wild rage in nature that was chained with the appearance of Man. Man appeared only at the *end* of the work of creation. A legend goes that the mate of the Leviathan was destroyed by God, otherwise those monsters would have ruined the world (*Baba Batra*). There is a profundity in these ideas, which—in an archaic language —anticipates what today has been affirmed by advanced science. In nature there is a wild untamed *rage*. One being is fighting the other, devouring the other. The fathomless magnitude of the galaxies, the raging speed of rays, the miraculously short lifetime of electrons also belong to this realm of sub-human rage. *Man* is the mighty *binder* of that sub-human realm. The NAME *Shaddai* indicates the majestic *Enough*, by which HE set bounds to the universe. HIS Shabbath overtakes even HIS work of creation.

The nations—*ha goyim—rage,* and rage they must, because they conceive themselves as being *natural,* as being the products of a natural process, and take great pride in it. What is biologically strong, has mostly expansionist urges. Israel is not a natural group but a founded unity. There is a profound difference between *goi* (nation) and *am* (people). *Am* is centered around HIM, it is neither a natural nor a political structure. Israel has been *extricated from nature.* This is Israel's unchangeable destiny and dignity. Being elevated above nature and nature's rage is the potential basis for *overcoming* this rage. Moreover, rage and fear are tied together; they are inseparable.

Is it really true that when fear is decreasing, crime is increasing? It may be true to a very limited degree. Fear is no deterrent to strong destructive impulses. Depth-psychology is aware of the fact that *"rage is a compensation for weakness."* Man is weak, as our Scriptures teach us. Viciousness develops as a counter-balance to our weakness or frustrations. Man feels weak just because he is uplifted above nature, and this in turn deprives him of the immediate surety which the animal possesses. The animal's not-inhibited strength is restricted in us. Our superiority is by the same token also our profoundest difficulty. The higher a being stands the more it is exposed to more challenging tasks and risks. What makes us weak is our *undecidedness* whether or not to accept a destiny that has been bestowed on us. As long as we are not aware of the infinitely higher powers that still are slumbering in us, we will remain weak.

Job, through the answer that GOD HIMSELF had given him, had to learn that his true genuine place was not in nature. GOD's question to Job: "Where wast thou when I created the universe?" *is the supreme answer*. Israel has been taught to live on a plane high above the wild rage of nature. Israel has been extricated from that twofold fear, to be either overpowered by nature or to be detached from nature. Israel *is not in need* of rage. The "nations" must rage, because they still rely on drawing their strength from nature; they feel weak when alienated from nature. Israel—on the other hand—is becoming weak by its *indecision*, whether or not to accept its destiny of being elevated above it.

Nations, power-groups, interests and privileges, as well as the religions, can never unite. *Peace* is not a political or organizational conception but a *Messianic* concept. This is why *Shalom* is also a Name of the *Messiah*. When David was asking why the nations rage, he added that "the kings and the rulers of the earth take counsel against HIM and HIS Messiah." (Teh. 2.2) Why? Because kings and rulers have to stand for the status quo. Theirs is the task of maintaining the given situation. However, no change more revolutionary is possible than to establish Peace. Since there is *no rage* in Israel, it is endowed with the potentiality of establishing PEACE.

A People Liberated from Magic Looks at Automation

It is said: "The Great Flood which had washed away a corrupted generation from the face of the earth, is called *mabul.*" This word means only a fullness, an abundance. Up to the last moment it was open to Man whether this abundance should come as blessing or as destruction. So it is also today. A fullness, an abundance is coming over mankind, but—just as then—it depends entirely on us, whether this will mean wealth or death. Why is this so? Why are we so utterly unable to master our own creations? What is wrong with us, producing the vicious circle into which our overwhelming technological triumphs are running? This is the vicious circle: The more power we create the more we become powerless. The miraculous creations of our minds and of our hands make us their slaves, even threaten to destroy us, physically, mentally, humanly. Can *Jewish Wisdom* illuminate the perplexities of the "Atomic Era," and even farther reaching, can it enlighten us in the coming era of *Automation?* We hold there is such a light.

Let us apply some Jewish fundamentals to the new and not yet fully realized implications of "Automation." What is emerging now dwarfs everything that technology has so far accomplished. Automation will make machines control machines, the acme of such super-machines being the "Electronic Brain." Man, step by step, will be eliminated from the production process. Already now these devices perform miraculous tasks. Day after day fantastic new devices are being invented, and soon all of our present technical equipment will become obsolete. We are not concerned here with the problem of "technological unemployment"; we are concerned with a much more severe problem: What will happen to Man? Will automation be a blessing? Will it—as many believe—provide Man with a life of plenty? Since the machines are doing the work for us, will they provide Man with leisure time? Will a chance be given to Man to strive for higher, nobler aims? We believe that this will not be so. It is naive to believe that abundance will come as a blessing rather than an annihilating *mabul.* Why?

The new *mabul*, the super-abundance in automation, will come to a totally unprepared and immature mankind. Between the upsurge of our inventions and our ethical and mental maturing lies an ever-widening gap of disharmony. Man—unprepared—equipped with ever more powerful tools cannot but worsen Man's plight. An old saying has it: "What can be worse than the right tool in the hand of the wrong man?" It is said that Bileam could not curse Israel, as the vicious Balak wanted him to do, "because there was no magic in Israel." What is magic? Magic is action inside of the actual falsehood of our life, *acting with the methods of the falsehood.* Which "falsehood"? "Idolatry!" the most basic of our human failures and perversions. The idolator bows before the unreal. But, "besides HIM, there is nothing that is real." It is the genuine Jewish attitude *not to bow before anything whatsoever.* The profundity of the decision between the two trees in paradise reveals that we have placed the unreal above ourselves, that we have sunk into thinghood, and that we have made a *thing* of ourselves. Therefore we are cut off from the Tree of Life. We have never eaten of it. We are not yet fortified enough to administer and to master the fullness of an earthly wealth.

Since we have sunk into magic, nothing but magic can come whatever we do. More magic will only create ever more magic, but never more life. That is why automation will not come to us as liberation. That is why it will not enable us, but will subdue us under the *golem* of mechanism, why it will make us stare with ever greater infatuation at the miracles, which science and technology are so admiringly creating. There will *not* be, as the foremost theoretician of automation, Norbert Wiener, put the problem: "a human use of human beings." Ever more we will become robots. Already now, at the very beginning of the "New Industrial Revolution," the first signs of psychiatric effects on man are reported. The threat of the automation era will even surpass the threat of the atomic era.

So what can be done? Can we, should we, do away with these miraculous inventions, which, in themselves, can at least carry the *potentialities of blessings?* No, we cannot, we should not, but the presupposition for it being a blessing is: *A Non-Magical Humanity.*

It is for this Messianic goal that *A Non-Magical People* has been created. It is for this goal of the humanization of humanity that a People "was extricated out of bondage" and "elevated above all languages" (above all verbiage of magic, into which even the religions relapsed). But this one People was educated—as it has been said—"to remove meticulously the last vestiges of magic from the *Halachah*." To redeem the wonders of Man's inventions from the power of magic, to avert a new negative *mabul*, what better advice could be given than to consult this millennial training and experience in a non-magical life, to consult the People which is free— at least potentially—of the Primal Bondage. "LO KESSEM B'ISRAEL." "There is no magic in Israel."

THE INFATUATION OF OUR TIME WITH MURDER

It is said: "He who hurts the dignity of a fellow-man, making his blood rush into his face, he has murdered him." Here a lesser act than killing is called "murder." The commandment which is on top of the second of the two Stone Tablets that carry the eternal Constitution and the sole Fundament of any enduring reality, must *not* be translated as: "Thou shalt not *kill*," but as: "Thou shalt not *murder*." The Hebrew language has different words for "to kill" and "to murder." The Torah makes allowance for the killing of animals, for the death penalty, even for wars, although the sanctity of life occupies a very high place; but what is meant in *this* commandment is the *sanctity of each man in his uniqueness*. Each and everyone has his place, provided for him in the universal concatenation of all beings and all things, each and everyone is irreplaceable, and these places are not exchangeable. It is said (*Shoftim*): "And everyone in the camp stood on his place." One can hardly say more. He who tries to usurp the ultimate place of his fellow man is a murderer. Even without killing him, he is a murderer. There is a touching ancient story of two sages who were executed at the time of the persecution of the Jews under the Roman Emperor Hadrian. On their way to the execution place, the one sage said to the other: "Why does this happen to us? Do console me, so that I may understandingly face my death." Answering, the other sage had only this to say: "Remember; did it happen perhaps that a supplicant came to ask you for help and you had him wait because you wanted to finish your meal, and he—while waiting—painfully felt his humiliation?" To this the first sage only answered: *"Thou hast consoled me."*

If such slight human neglect already is called murder, if such slight transgression *already* shows the root of our disrespect for the legitimate place of our fellow man, this may give us a clue *to understand the infatuation of our time with murder.* Murder is in ourselves. It is an almost unconscious fascination, a longing for something that lies repressed in our souls, and which is all the more fascinating when we see it actually happen. This infatuation with murder must be understood as a half-conscious wish-fulfillment of a suppressed urge, akin to the "death-wish," Freud's tremendous discovery of a profound "NO" to life, deep down in our subconscious soul, breaking through into conscious life at countless spots of weak resistance.

Our actual conscious life and the actual organization of our society is based on *three deep-rooted urges of a negative nature: fear, sex and competition.* The relation between fear and sexuality has been masterly explored by Freud. The competitive or fighting urges are equally related to the general denominator of these three, namely—death. Sex and death are akin because the sex urges solely serve the maintenance of the *species,* and *not of the individual,* which is sacrificed for that purpose, a mere *germ.* The individual "dies", as it were, into the species in each sex-act.

It is most indicative that our time is still very touchy about describing sexual acts in literature or elsewhere, but there is not the slightest objection to the description of murder in the tiniest detail, even greatly enjoying it, and it is of course a big business. Why? Because our present social order cannot afford this safety valve; but eventually it must make a stand *against the Three Jewish Absolutes,* these Minimum Demands of the Jewish Way of Life—the three *absolute prohibitions of: idolatry, perversity, murder.* These three are never to be transgressed, even if the price to pay is one's own life. *These Three Absolute Prohibitions* are an indivisible unity, and transgression is tantamount to extinction. To let sexuality into the open to be purged there in the bright light of consciousness from perversions would mean giving up a most effective fear-stimulus, as psychoanalysis has clearly demonstrated. But to give up fear is precisely what our present order of things cannot afford to do without seriously undermining its fundaments—for to close up the sources of fear would help us to bow no longer before the irrealities, it would eventually *end* idolatry.

Yet we can least afford to do this since that would mean depriving ourselves of taking refuge in this effective defense-mechanism against the *Three Absolute Prohibitions*. It would mean recognizing the *golem* as a *golem* and the *mamser* as a *mamser*. However, we are in such panic-stricken anxiety, trying to *preserve* the spook and to *remain* a *mamser* rather than to be human that the majestic word on the top of the Second Stone Tablet disturbs us deeply. A murderous soul can but stare in fascination at its own guilt-feelings. Because Jewish Thinking understands the deep kinship of idolatry—perversity—murder—and how they condition each other, it also understands the roots of our murder-infatuation, and therefore is equipped to show the way out.

The Fallacy of "Fighting Anti-Semitism"

It is said (B'midb. 22) that when Bileam went out using all the power of his black magic to curse Israel, God spoke to him, saying: "Thou shalt not curse them, for they are blessed." And to Abraham HE revealed (Ber. 12): "He who blesses you, is blessed, and he who curses you, is cursed." This should suffice.

To "fight" anti-Semitism should be left to the Gentiles. It is a disease in their camp. But the Jews may support noble Gentiles who fight anti-Semitism in their own ranks. However, one can have no illusions about the result as long as things are left fundamentally unchanged. Why is this so? Where does the fallacy of it stem from? A predominantly apologetic movement can never be convincing. It does not establish its own position, but relates itself merely to the evaluation given by others. Even modest attempts to dispel

persistent lies and fictions, e.g., "all Jews are rich, Jews are an inferior race, the Jews are planning a global conspiracy," and the like,
have hardly accomplished any tangible results. The Jews are still
uncanny aliens among the nations, still an obscure group. Slight
improvements or minor mitigations of discrimination are quickly
wiped out when a nation goes through a period of lesser prosperity,
or through critical times; and when a nation reaches the "power
stage" in its history, which always indicates the end-stage of a
national evolution, then the antagonism between the Jew and
his host-nation rapidly increases. It is in these periods that the relatively quieter periods of co-existence are superceded by a violent rejection or even elimination of the Jews. It is in these periods that
the opposition of the power-system to the Jews—and of the Jews
in the power-system—reaches the culmination point. These insights, which we learn from history, are also not being applied
in the "fight anti-Semitism" movements. These naively believe that
the whole problem of the millennial hostility against the Jews is a
mere fictitious problem, a problem of prejudices, of demagoguery,
of minority issues and the like, which will be overcome by correct information.

Since, therefore, the true issue is not raised, and mostly not
even seen, it is obvious why attempts to overcome anti-Semitism
must remain fallacious. The only hope for change would lie in the
awareness—resolutely affirmed—that there is a very real issue.
More—that this issue is a most fundamental challenge which, by
necessity, must stir up Man's deepest passions. From the very
beginning, the radical Monotheism of the Hebrew Scriptures and
the conception of a "Theocracy where nobody should rule but
HE," was a steady challenge to the "normal" ways of life. Since
ancient times, up to our days, the Jew was the omni-present, never-
disappearing admonisher, exposing a falsity which men are only too
anxious to perpetuate. The radical NO of the Jews to the falsities
of paganism, to the worshipping of nature and the bowing before
the powers, the NO to the perversities of our social order, the
NO to all magical or orgiastic cultures, is "the" issue, which separates
men from each other. All the other demarcation lines are fictitious,
compared with the one basic division. This division should be kept

alive, we pray, to the very end. Never did the Jew allow the evading of this theme of the history of mankind. Wherever and whenever it was attempted, the Jew blocked the way.

Such attitudes must necessarily arouse a passionate antagonism, a feeling of guilt that tries to submerge itself in forgetfulness is thus steadily and disturbingly stirred up, and is psychologically mightier than all attempts to persuade the world that the Jewish aspect of life is "coordinatable." However, this persuasion fails and must fail, because it does not consider the repressed guilt-feeling of the world, which needs to escape into anti-Semitism and cannot yet afford to give up so effective a psychological defense-mechanism. The Jews will not allow the world to forget the six million murdered Jews, when the world now wants to blot out the memory of what has been done.

What then is a better way than persuading people that there is no "real" Jewish question. The better way would be: state the issue, stand for the issue, and with determination! When Israel left Egypt, transcending the "house of bondage," when the sea was split before Israel, this was not a fight, this was an Exodus. The fight was God's fight. When Israel was told: *"Taharishun"*—"Be silent," not a passive muteness was meant, but the majestic silent tranquility, peacefully proclaiming its truth by its very presence, as the starry heavens speak out what they are, majestically silent.

Do not trust to trying to persuade men to accept a fallacy. Do trust in truth. It is Jewish to trust in the Greatness of Man. Surely, Men will understand.

RISING ABOVE THE "HOW TO—"

The word "Hineni"—"Here I am," is one of the keywords of the Hebrew language. When the Call came from HIM to the Fathers they at once proclaimed their readiness, and not even a split-second was in between the Call and their acceptance. Had they allowed even a fraction of a moment to be between the Call and their acceptance, nothing might have followed the Call.

This is the secret of all higher action that aims at higher goals rather than mere practical goals. There is a way that supersedes the way of practical daily life. Practical life has to *sustain* and to preserve life, but it cannot *elevate* life. To lift our life to higher regions is not a matter of being "practical." All practicalism is merely a pre-requisite for a higher efficiency of Man. Moreover, without supe-rior aims even our practical aims are running into vicious circles, even-tually frustrating us. As it is said: *"Ein kemach, ein Torah"* (no bread, no Torah), but it also says: *"Ein Torah, ein kemach"* (no Torah, no bread).

Therefore, this higher action is not the result of a long calculat-ing of pros and cons, it is not a result of skill, of a "how to," or of organizing, managing or making; it is immediate, it comes as a *leap*. And this leap is—as some deeper insights know—an act tran-scending consciousness. One is aware of the old and the new position, but not of the "in between," and it is good that this is so. That the steps of higher ways are strangely unconnected, that they are not pedestrian, that there is no "how to" between the "in" and the "out" of our great perplexities, that there is no "way" to the superior and higher abodes—this is the meaning of the *"Hineni."* Such insight is also not unknown to the highest peaks of Chinese Philosophy. Of course, practical action is gradual. To build a house, to perform sur-gery, to run a grocery store, one has to know the "how to." But when it comes to higher actions, to actions which transform, transfigure, transcend all practical aims, these actions happen in immediacy. All true Jewishness is a form of immediacy, of a "Now." "If not now—when?" goes the well-known word (*Pirke Avoth*). *Ematai?* When? The Jew is always "a Jew—Now."

"Hineni" means, there are no *intermediaries* in Hebrew wis-dom. Between HIM and Man is solely the word. It is said: (Shemoth 33) "There is a place next to ME." (*Iti*) "Next to ME." No fusion! No fusion of GOD and Man is possible, only *Nearness*. Nearness is free of the paralyzing condition imposed by the "between" and the "how to." No Intermediaries! This is one of the points of profoundest difference between Jewish teachings and the various re-ligions. The "angels"—probably imported from dualistic systems into the Biblical system—are messages rather than messengers. They

have no reality of their own, they are only "functions," and each one has one single function only. For the Jews there are no "beings" to turn to, no saints to pray to, nor any mediating institutions. This immediacy, which makes no allowance whatsoever for "in betweens" when it comes to superior actions, establishes a spontaneity above all "practical," "technical" action, and above all, any "how to's." It establishes an autonomy of Man's more sublime faculties over and above the broad stress of our daily practical actions. For us today, actions other than practical are not feasible, but we begin to realize that this bare practicalism, stripped of the envelopes of higher meaning, could bring us to annihilation. We have lost the sight of the exit. But this exit is hidden in the immediacy, which is above all "in-betweenness." The normalationist will point to the unrealistic hope of leaving behind practicalism; but the Jew may point to his experience in history, that even a touch of pure *truth* —"pure" meaning without any mixture of falsity—is stronger. The "Learning Jew" renews daily his awareness of the exits, which can be reached without the detour through the maze of things.

Where the Bread Is Seen by HIM

It is said: "And put the bread before My Countenance—steadily." Bread, the very symbol of human food was to be put before HIM steadily, "on the Pure Table." (Shemoth 25, 30.) (Vayikra 24, 6.) Bread is here not just an industrial product to be bought and to be sold, but *to be seen by HIM*. Having its genuine place on "Israel's Pure Table," is the deepest root for being provided with our daily bread. (In the Hebrew view, the table does not merely hold something, but OFFERS.) So it was gloriously conceived in the ritual of the "*Lechem Panim*," in the Tent Of Meeting With HIM, in the desert, and later on in the Temple. This surpasses all the propositions of economy and politics. The table whereon it was put, served as the paradigma of the correct unity of consuming and purity. "Seen by HIM." So, as is said: "with everything we consume *Now*, we take away from our share in the world to come," and: "to make a living is a greater miracle than the cleavage of the Red Sea," these words challenge the very fundament of our economic system and our production process, and our callousness to what is legitimate in the Divine Light. Just as the bread, so the light —in form of the Menorah—was also put before HIM steadily (*tamid*). As in *Bereshith*: "HE saw the light, *and it was good.*" (HE saw "that" it was good, is a wrong translation.)

We trust in what we see. We are not aware that we *are seen. That we are seen* is deeply established in the meaning of one of the Names of God, the Name *Makom* ("Place"). "HE is the place of the world." Everything is "placed," is not resting in itself, by itself. A very great vision! There is this insight at the bottom of Einsteinian Relativity also. Why could not genuine science and Divine Truth meet in harmony! The universe we live in is not a closed room; one could better compare it to a glass-house; it is transparent, wide-open, it opens up in the *Makom*. Everything in the universe *is steadily seen*, nothing is hidden, nothing is private. This is *not a private* world. How the *seen* life differs from the lone, private life, which thinks it is all by itself! Our acquisitive society— to borrow a term from the renowned sociologist Tawney—has separated the entire realm of action from its "containment" in the *Makom* (Place), so that practical life and the production process —hiding from Him, as it were—are running solely on their own, managed only by organizational and technological considerations. That is why the end will be demonic. Calvin's religious axioms, which partly promoted the modern philosophy of economics, are dominated by the idea (nowhere supported by the Holy Script) that Man is lost, that mankind is a "mass of perdition," is given up. Consequently, "success" has been made the measure for judging men. But the *Jewish view* is that light, and bread, gain their continuing reality only in "being seen steadily," in being placed on the "Pure Table." Bread is lifted up from merchandise to *"Lechem Panim"*—"most Holy to HIM." No comment is needed to see how deeply such a controversial view differs from "normalcy." However —"all controversies undertaken for the sake of *HIS TRUTH* will lead to PEACE (*Pirke avoth*)."

To Suspend Mountains on a Hair

A widely known story goes that once a pagan came to Hillel with a quest: "If you can explain to me what are the teachings of your Torah, *while I am standing on one foot,* I may become a Jew." Hillel at once answered: "What is hateful unto thee do not do unto thy fellow man; this is the entire Torah, the rest is its interpretation, *go and learn.*" Precisely this is the definition of ethics, as given two thousand years later by one of the greatest philosophers, Kant. So Hillel accepted the demand for an answer, which is quick and short, but he did not give up the *basic* Jewish demand "to learn." The chance to encourage an initial awakening should never be missed, even "while standing on one foot." Everything begins with the "readiness." It must never be rejected. For, as a profound Talmudic insight states: "Readiness leads to purity." And one could add: purity leads to unity, to an inner unification. Only from an undivided mind radiates a power, which is free of all destructive effects.

A touching story tells of the Baalshem: When the sparks of all the future souls, contained in Adam, were confronted with the forbidden tree in paradise, the tree wherein all division originated, the Baalshem's soul did not *eat* of its fruits. So he remained undivided, and his undivided soul never lost the primal joy of life, which he radiated to all.

Where there is *Serisuth*—the readiness to accept the Jewish destiny, then even in the darkest hours there is still hope. It is worthwhile to remember something that happened in Germany when the Nazi persecution of the Jews started. A deep despair had befallen them. One day there appeared an article in a Zionist newspaper, written by a Zionist leader, Robert Weltsch, carrying the caption: "Wear it with pride, *this Yellow Patch.*" It has been said that this call prevented multitudes of Jews from committing suicide. Says the Talmud: "What the vicious prepare, the righteous will wear." Suddenly the Jews understood that the "Yellow Patch" attached to them as a sign of defamation through the centuries, was the badge of highest honor. It was a moment of "Serisuth," of this ever *renewed acceptance* of a sublime destiny, bestowed on the Jews.

A wise man of our time once said he would gladly give up encyclopaedias full of knowledge, for the one little word, which might again give him hope for Man. There are Hebrew words of just such miraculous power. One such word is: *Hineni, Here I am.* It is a proclamation of utter readiness. It does not allow even a split moment's time between the Call, which comes to Man, and his answer. In between the hearing and the accepting there should be no "how to"; no meditating process. The *Hineni* of Abraham, of Moses, is *absolute immediacy.* It is the starting point of all aiming at higher goals. In a Kabbalistic theory, the entire world was created from one point, a theory which, strangely enough, is also to be found in modern physics. From a right beginning a true world may arise. Or—a very different witness, Napoleon, said: "First one has to engage oneself, and then one has to see."

To apply this to a very actual controversy: In the new State of Israel the question was raised: "Are we Israelis still Jews?" If they were not (but they surely are), the Jews in all the countries could very well answer: "What then is still our interest in the State of Israel?" However, a better answer is possible. Supposing that many Israelis gave up much of their Jewishness, was it not done *just because* they wanted to restore what they earnestly believed to be true Jewishness, namely the togetherness with the people? Look at what they regained in the Kibbutzim. Yet we must not be unaware of enemy number one. A greater enemy than all the Nebukadnezars in history is: NORMALIZATION. "Let us be like all the nations." (Sam. 1.)

But—where there is readiness, not all is lost. We venture to say, that there is much renewed *Serisuth* among the Jews. Look at it carefully even while standing on one foot.

IN THE HUTS AND NOT IN THE PALACES

There is a saying that "only the lowly understand the Torah fully." And another: "With everything we consume now, we have already consumed our share in the world to come." This means there is something problematic in our consuming and owning. And, with a melancholic smile, still another word has it that *"parnassah* (to make a living) is a greater miracle than the cleavage of the Red Sea." All these words put a big question-mark behind what seems to be the simplest pre-requisite of life. Why?

Here we are touching on a deep root of Jewishness, challenging the very fundament of life. As the Torah sees it, Man failed at the very beginning, when he was confronted with the basic decision, to choose between life and death. Man did not choose life but death (Ber. 3). It is the story of this primal tragedy, the story of the *cleavage* wrought by Man upon the original work of creation, and of the cleavage Man has caused in himself. His brokenness may be called the "basic schizophrenia" of human nature. It is also called *kitzuz b'netioth,* the separation Man made between the two trees in paradise, the tree of life and the tree of knowledge, thus destroy-ing the primal unity. Henceforth all acquisition, all owning, all consuming, even the plain fact that we need food and shelter was no longer the *legitimate basis* of life. It thus became the *illegiti-mate anticipation* of the condition in the "world to come," which will again be free of the corruption wrought by us. "Now we are all as an unclean thing and our justice like filthy rags." (Isaiah 64.)

Therefore *legitimate* life is in exile. Or more precisely, with Man, the Shechinah (God's presence on earth) is in exile. With the exiles, with the homeless, with the outcasts, with the unsettled, with the lowly, the Shechinah is wandering through history. But the Shechinah is not with those in power. So, the restoration of life to its divine legitimacy—the *tikkun* (to use a kabbalistic term) must come from the lowly, must originate in the people. It cannot come from any privileged stratum. The remedy for the basic schizo-phrenia can only come from below. What wields power, or what re-lies on power cannot restore the primal Divine Reality. But the *mehiruth,* the readiness of the lowly can restore it. The *call from the depths,* the *Itharutha dil-tata* calls forth the impulse from above. Sociologically seen, there can hardly be a more consequential idea.

The lowly do not by their own volition partake in the falsehood.

They are drawn into it just because of their powerlessness, which is also their innocence. In Hannah's prayer (Sam. 1,2) we read: "The bows of the mighty men are broken and the beggar lifted up from the dunghill, by HIM." The social laws of the Torah, as the great periodical equalization of the Jobel Year, as the prohibition of taking or giving interests, as the law that the land belongs solely to HIM, are points of vehement resistance down the centuries; they are, however, an intrinsic part of the Bible. The Messiah is described by Isaiah (in the famous chapter 53) as the despised, suffering Man. So, this early Biblical conception of messianic suffering does not originate—as it was claimed—in Christianity, which later on delegated the very concrete suffering of the people to a vicarious substitute.

Whatever the function of the "institutions, states or churches may be, all officialdom has merely a managerial but no messianic faculty. Therefore, the messianic people, Israel is not just one among these many institutions and groups, it is not *coordinatable*. One of the greatest sociologists of modern times, Max Weber, called Israel a "pariah people." This has been misunderstood as a derogative remark, though it had been meant as highest praise. It was an outcast people, forged into unity and shaped *in the desert*. In the desert *they lived in huts*. The wisdom and the purity of the huts anticipates—as it were—year by year, in a joyful festival, a harvesting freed of the frightful curse of Genesis (Ber. 3): "Cursed is the ground for thy sake." Note this: the *ground*, not Man.

Knowingly and wisely one of our sages said: "The more sublime a system is the less 'power' it has." The Talmud knew that of all our passions only the lust for power never reaches satiety. *This is why all power must go insane.* Judaism has never been a power system. This is why Israel's Soul remained sane in all its wandering through history. This is why the answer to our great anxiety will not come from the palaces, it will come from the huts.

The Returning Jew

It is said: "At the place where the *Baale Teshuvah* can stand, not even the Zaddikim can stand." This means: those who learn to turn around, out of the confusion, out of the falsehood can reach heights, which the upright but unproblematic cannot reach. This sounds hard, but it gives us a clue to detect those with whom the momentum lies, who still are capable of reaching the open road again, where Man can advance. He who is honest knows that all the solutions offered today are insufficient to help us in our perplexities. There is either a panicky fury to keep the status quo, or there is such a "change" that leaves Man's basic perplexities unchanged. But where is a "Messianic change"? Where is the lost momentum to be found? A great sentence may answer: "Ain massol l'Jisrael." This means: Israel is under no 'constellation,' under no domination of fate. To be a Jew means to be free. Yet—is this so in actual life? At least the inner core preserved an initial spontaneity. At least a nucleus had never broken away from the Divine Heritage. This nucleus did not bow to corruption, did not fall victim to the confusion, did not for a moment abandon the Messianic Destiny of the Jewish people. When tested they died rather than surrender. But there were others, not less faithful, devoted and observant, yet deeply *immersed* in the life of the world, with all its conflicts, might and splendor. Who, after all, could live in this ever narrowing planet without being touched by this life of our time! Nobody can escape the challenge Man is faced with today: the challenge that comes from science, from the psychoanalytical unmasking of the human soul, from the vicious circle of commercialized life, from the supremacy of technology over the humanities and the threat of automation, transforming men into robots. In this irresistible development the religious feeling is almost blotted out. Worse than the threat of physical annihilation is the inner emptiness, plunging us into an abysmal global anxiety.

The Jews did not remain untouched by all this. And those Jews who are not fortified to a very high degree are thus breaking away from their Divine Heritage. This is so also in the new State of Israel—meant as a bulwark against this trend. However—behold the *Baale Teshuvah,* the returning Jews! They do what even the innermost Midst did not do, *they reverse this going away from the center.* This "turning around" is not a backward but an upward movement! Certainly, no Return would be possible, were it not for the firm center to which the Jew could turn as to his "deepest home."

The specific task of the returning Jew is to resist assimilation without falling into the fallacy of remaining indifferent to the development of the modern world, to its greatness but also its frightening consequences. He knows that the only hope for the Jew and for Man generally, lies in reaching a position *far beyond and above the present situation, overtaking this crisis of humanity.*

This the Jew did down the millennia, going through many cultures, deeply immersed in them, and again emerging from exodus to exodus, each time reaching a higher stage on his ascent. Overtaking these cultures and yet preserving *their values,* he often served as their Ark.

Today culture everywhere reaches its borderline, and our ways of life remain bogged down entirely within these borders. The inner hostilities are great but all are standing and fighting futilely on the same ground. The Jew has a specific faculty for overtaking the global crisis, because this global crisis is the ultimate showdown of all "magical culture," and the soul of Israel is redeemed from magic. This faculty to emerge from the general confusion is strangely lacking in our time.

The movement of the returning Jew towards the Midst creatively shifts the problems of our time into totally new aspects, leading us again to the open road. This road is blocked by the "normalization Jew." But the "returning Jew" is a Habakuk, meaning "the Devoted Embracer." In his *embracing* he *overtakes* the falsehoods, and in his returning he *embraces* the *Midst,* which in the end will *embrace him.*

HEAR THE MIGHTY CALL: FOCUS THE PEOPLE!

The sound of the *Shofar* is breathtaking because it breaks forth—from fathomless depths—the primordial experience of the Founding of the Jewish People, slumbering deep down within the Jewish souls, breaks like a storm into our conscious life. It is the mighty call that the people shall *arise and gather*. The dying Jaakov, in his last blessing (Ber. 49) set the theme of the history of the Jews: "Gather." "Hear." "Unite." "Gather"—for breaking up the tents and ascending to a new exodus. "Hear"—the highest faculty in Man to transcend himself. "To hear" is the secret of Jewishness. "Unite" (*hikabzu*)—in an everlasting Kibbuz.

The Jews are a people. Detached from it the Jew vanishes. Detached from it, Jewish wisdom evaporates into a mere religious denomination. Those who deny that the Jews are a people are either ignorants or escapists. The Bible is the very story of the building up, shaping, and educating a people, setting it apart from all the nations and cultures. The Bible describes its growth, how it was tested, punished, blessed, and forged in the incandescent Divine fire. It tells us of its relapses, and of its fearless readiness to make its way through the tribulations and dangers of history to the Messianic end, so that the history of this people became "Universal History." Moses did not only bring the Torah to the people, he formed a people for the Torah. And in the people's midst there was HE. Said Moses: "If Thou goest not in our midst, blot me out of Thy Book." HE destined the Fathers—Abraham, Jizchak and Jaakov—to become the founders of a people. Emphatically the Holy Script describes its evolution in terms of genealogies. Relentlessly did Esra's and Nehemia's radicalism protect the purity of this genealogy.

Compare what the great early Americans called "Ultimate persons." Not the "private" individual, only the wide-open transprivate individual is a true person. The highest demand of the Bible, "To Be Holy," is made to the *People*. "Ye the People shall be holy unto Me." It was a People that went from exodus to exodus, from land to land, from ghetto to ghetto. For the sake of the People they gave their lives by the thousands in the *Kidush Ha Shem*, rather than betray their Messianic destiny. A People created the Talmud, the Kabbalah, Hassidism and took upon itself the rigor of the Halakhah. Those who say the Jews are nothing but one of the hundreds of "religious denominations," are free to reject the Bible but not free to distort the Bible.

All collectives, however beautiful, however useful or dignified they may be, are relative collectives. Only a togetherness that is focused around Him has a "midst" and can be called an "Absolute Collective." A human togetherness where nobody rules but HE, is called "Theocracy." The struggle between the Great Powers and Theocracy is the genuine issue of history. No relative community, ideological or practical, can make absolute claims. The Founding Fathers of this country said that one's first obligation is to the voice of conscience. No honest man can ever be certain that he may not come face to face with a conflict of conscience. The devotion of the Jews to the lands wherever they lived was deep and strong, they never failed their country, probably because they knew an ultimate devotion.

It has been said: "To be uprooted from the people" is absolute extinction, it is *Death Eternal*; but *Life Eternal* was conceived as being gathered into the indestructible concatenation of the people. There is the abode of that future when "death will be swallowed up in victory" (Isaiah), for death is not intrinsic to the world. Not in endless prolongation of individual life but in swinging out into the *Absolute Collectivity* lies our hope for immortality. If the people is lost, deathless life is lost. Never was the danger of Man's sinking into nothingness greater than today. Never was a more radical togetherness achieved than in the course of the history of the Jews. The order of Israel's camp in the desert was of a Divine Structure. It was arranged around the *Ohel Moed*, The Tent of Meeting with HIM. "Behold the Hut of God among men." It was commanded: "So as they encamp so they should march on." (B'midbar 12,17.) Resting or marching on—not for one moment should the people suspend the fundamental structure of its Founding. And *Thus* we must pursue our Messianic Way.

Terua!   Tekia!   Hear!

FOCUS THE PEOPLE!

Why the Jews Do Not Utter His Ineffable Name

"Hear Oh Israel"—this word is in itself a whole philosophy. But how can we "hear" in the bedlam of today! We are *deaf*. Not open any longer to being addressed, we have forgotten how to speak, we are getting *mute*. That the "word" is dying is an apocalyptic warning. The words of the Torah are holy. Our words are trade-labels for merchandise, hollow and ultimately mendacious—but a profound chastity of speech is Israel's heritage. The Commandment: "Thou shalt not take the Name of God in vain" means that HIS Name should not be attached to emptiness, should not endow an irreality with reality, of which HE is the owner. Yet—to attach HIS Name to falsehood is the very viciousness of our time. To us today it is not given to communicate with HIM, as did the Fathers and the Prophets. We can neither hear HIM nor address HIM. We cannot honestly say "HE," and therefore we cannot honestly say "I" either, because only the addressed "I" is a genuine "I." "I" is not—as we wrongly believe—privacy. Such a private "I" does not have a genuine "Thou," nor has it a genuine "We." Today our honesty is preserved only in our silence. His ineffable Name is silent in the Jewish people, though everything and everybody is named after Him. Israel, the surname of the Jews, proclaims "HE RULES" (not only He "exists"). We do not name Him, He names us.

The official religions talk "about" Him in an easy way. This easy talk is called theology. They talk as if He were a calculable factor, nicely integrated as the pinnacle of our actual world. But when He is present He disintegrates our falsehood. As the Scripture says: "I will come up in the midst of thee in a moment and consume thee." (Shemoth 33.) Yet it is also said that He can dwell amidst the people in all their impurity. But He will dwell there as an incandescent fire, as a revolutionary challenge. He is not a convenient pattern to drown our unrest, *HE makes problems emerge*. Here we are touching the roots of our present alienation from religion—theology is the reason. God as the pinnacle of this actual world of ours means to seal the falsehood with the NAME. It so happens that just the most devout religiosity revolts against

this Divine sanctioning of a fallacious world, and breaks away from
the official religions. Not much of militant atheism remains with
us, for *our era* has turned atheistic altogether. However, the Jewish
position is by no means vulnerable to this general trend, because
Jewish faith is not a theology. Theology is a camouflaged version of
atheism. No faith has a better chance for surviving this crisis
of religion than the Jewish faith. The Jewish chastity before the
Name is of an utter sensitiveness and is setting the Jews apart. The
true climax in the Jesus Story came when he pronounced the Name.
In the silence of Israel His Name is preserved.

What answer then to the crisis of religion? Reverse its basic
question: not—what kind of God belongs to this our actual world,
but what kind of world belongs to Him? No addressing Him in terms
of speech which is a mute speech. It is said: The *Shechinah* is in exile and so are we, with her. A great representative of this tragedy is
the poet Franz Kafka. A modern Job, he describes in sober words
the demonic situation which is ours (using a Hebrew term—the
"mamser" world), a world in which HE is absent, but all things
cry out His absence, thus proclaiming His ultimate presence.

The story of the Babylonian Tower (Gen. 11) built by the
"generation of dispersion" tells us how they wanted "to make a name
for themselves." So they pulled down the "Name," the keyword of
language and attached the Name to nothingness, to the emptiness
of fame. Then the entire edifice of speech collapsed; speech withered away. (No one could any longer understand the other.)
And—the story of the Golem: This raging monster, bent on destroying the world! What was the secret of his power? He carried
the Name under his tongue. When the Name was taken from under
his tongue, he crumbled to dust. It teaches us: Take the Name
from under the tongue of the monster, and you will stop the threatening annihilation.

It is said: *Lo sh'mo bo sh'mo.* Where His Name is silent, His
Name may be deep inside. In Israel's silence there is the place
where still one can *hear.*

The Great Hour of American Jewry Is Near

"The Golden Chain" of the Jewish Tradition has never been broken. Nor did the Jews on their way through history ever fail to go to stages higher and higher. Said the Zohar: "The Holy Torah would wither away if it *were* not continually *enhanced*." Let us start with one of those words that have fortified our identity down the millennia, the question to Man: "Where art thou?" (Ge. 3,9.) This is the *basic call* of the Bible, the call to an utter readiness, to an ever new awareness of "Where are we?" At each stage of their history the Jews have gloriously answered it. And this mighty call *now is coming to the American Jew.* Is he ready? Was it enough to celebrate the "Tercentenary" by praising the successes of our integration into American life? Yet—what of our contributions in these three centuries to building up Israel's eternal destiny? And what is the specifically Jewish impact on American civilization? A little amendment to this impact: Columbus, the Marrano (he most certainly was), made the amazing statement in his Diaries that he started on his voyage just two days after the expulsion of the Jews from Spain. So connecting the end of the Spanish with the beginning of the American stage of Jewish history an almost mystical historical continuity was established. And this: The acknowledged indebtedness of the Founding Fathers to the radicalism of the Old Testament in shaping the Great American Dream. Would not the finest celebration have been to rise to the awareness that the great task of the American Jew *is still to come?*

It is not so that all the Jews outside of the land of Israel are doomed to wither away. Zion and the diaspora are an indivisible unity. As it was said: "Zion is the midst of the world". Of the *world!* Zion is not a lonely island. And the *Golus* is not sickness but profoundest destiny. Even the very State of Israel is still in *Golus*. American Jewry is the biggest settlement of Jews in history. And with it goes the mighty responsibility of responding to the eternal Biblical Call of answering the anxious question of this frightful hour: Can Man survive? Is it worthwhile to survive? A Jewish answer *must* be given in this most crucial moment of Man's existence on earth.

But American Jewry is not *only* important because of its bigness. It is a special task, for it has been free of persecutions. (Discrimination is not persecution. There was no need for *Kiddush HaShem.*) Out of his own spontaneity the American Jew can accept his Jewish destiny, he can do it with joy and not with tears. *However, is he ready?* Always when the Jews failed to embrace their messianic destiny, the end was disaster. The tradition teaches: When the Jewish people were standing at Mount Sinai God held the mountain suspended over their heads and spoke: "Accept my Torah or it will be your grave." The Jews accepted, and thus they rose to the highest degree of freedom. To understand the paradox that necessity coming from HIM is utter freedom, is to understand the deepest mystery of Jewish faith.

Mightily were the Jews tested in all periods of their history and in *all* the lands where they lived. Ultimately there is no escape from being a Jew. This is the law of the Jewish history. On Israel's way mistakes are deadly. All the nations can get away with great sins. Take the Germans. No so the Jews. And assimilation—it always failed. Take the German Jews. The history of the German Jews was glorious. Only that many conscious German Jews believed that the German and the Jewish culture could be blended, was such a deadly mistake. Why repeat fallacies?

The American Jew will be graced to become the harbinger of Israel's next great historical step if he *affirms* and even *enhances* his identity rather than gradually giving it up. Not by conveying our Jewish wisdom in the vocabulary of the present global confusion, but by using *our own vocabulary*, in order to dissolve the confusion can we render a service to this country. The technological evolution, the industrialization and its social consequences have reached the borderline where a showdown is imminent. Now this country is on the furthermost front of the apocalyptic crisis of our time and is bearing the brunt of the global anxiety. Today, at the acme of its long development "magical culture" is running in vicious circles. Judaism is the only determined *anti-magical* way of life, and therefore it can overtake the anxiety which paralyzes mankind. The demand of the hour is: Devotion (*devekuth*), Readiness (*mehiruth*), Awareness (*ajecka*), and to discover the deepest roots of the unconquerable joy of the Jews. It is said: The *Shechinah* does not dwell with sad souls.

Sidereal Birth—Excerpts/ 1910

Thou, Thou End of the World

The wisdom of the deed that takes the breath away we make known today; and never were there more joyful tidings, for we proclaim the end of all finiteness and the beginning of boundless journeying. We shall show how in time to come action can never consist in making our worldly dwelling more and more comfortable. Not housing oneself in comfort, but limitless journeying is what we are now striving for. The concept of unending progress will no longer satisfy us, for we shall recognize that the world cannot progress forever, but if we do not wish to be suffocated at the world's zenith then an unheard-of newness must come to pass, something that is more glorious than all that has ever been. *The world must come to an end, but this can no longer frighten us.* To the end we utter the ardent: Thou, Thou! And this ardor for the end makes our time—which we recognize as the world's zenith—an event at once so ecstatic and so overwhelming that nothing in the past compares with it.

Our time is the turning-point where God-likeness is not only an image in our intellect but takes the form of action. All mundane narrowness ended, we shall advance from it to the deed. And all the abundance of temporal possessions we shall incorporate in God-like vibrancy, rescuing ourselves from the depth of nature and the abyss of matter and death.

We shall rise above nature and above the world into the realm of perfection, and all depths and heights we shall bring into the new at-one-ment. To achieve the unheard-of deed we shall expand ourselves, seraph-like, in embraces burning with love. In holy poverty we shall renounce the limitation of our little personality, this merely mechanical, as yet lifeless ego in order to gain our higher seraphic self, which is not subject to death, but partakes of all that is divine and will redeem the silent depths.

Above our culture, which must exhaust itself and does not rise forever, there will emerge the new culture of the sidereal birth, which *is* capable of rising forever. It will not draw the height of the Godhead into the narrow confines of the personality in a mere image, but will *act* like the Godhead by breaking through and perfecting the temporal. This new culture will pour the limited ego forth into the heights in flaming vitality, in sidereal birth, star-like above all stars.

Noon-tide Terror

More frightful than the terror of night is the terror at noon, when in the fiery heat every object lies sharply outlined, when the day can rise no more and in the mid-day everything is at its height. Such noon-tide terror our time is experiencing today. It is no ordinary affliction from which we suffer, as any time might make us suffer. It is the most extreme, the most frightful suffering, the suffering of the uttermost limitation, of finiteness, of death.

Utter exhaustion is the secret of our time. Yet we shall see again and again that this time is nevertheless not a time of pettiness or decadence, but the mightiest of world-changes, because today something new will come to pass, unheard-of through all the aeons; for the cause of the exhaustion is *that the world is at its noon-tide height.*

It seems, indeed, as though life never pulsed more furiously than in our day. Yet everywhere we behold the end. When nothing in the old order can satisfy us, we must seek the entirely new, new powers, new horizons, for the whole world has grown old and has become too narrow; and this is what makes our time so great. As our external culture has risen to such an immensity, with it has vanished the last hope that it can ever bring into existence the hoped-for Paradise. With it has risen only terror, new immeasurable terror. We believe no longer in the liberating mission of technical progress, civilization, medicine and the sciences. If all the ideals of this culture were realized, what then? We do not believe that the eternal human questions, the eternal human tragedy would be one whit nearer solution. Nor do we believe any longer that salvation can come through all the reforms and social revolutions, or through any art of living, or through all the parties and sects that commend themselves to us.

We shall see that all these are indeed necessary halting-places in the life of humanity, but never, never can they lead us to that unheard-of newness. Ever around us declines the vehemence of nature that before had goaded us on. We master nature so that our life may become more tranquil and more secure. Everything smoothed out, all diversity abolished, that is the tendency of our time. The earth has been explored and has grown small, nature lies robbed of her gods, and now that we are grown to manhood the religions and the ideas of God and Paradise seem childish to us. And we *have* grown to manhood. We cannot become children again. We see how the races are mingling and obliterating each other. The distinctive national characteristics are fading away.

Even the mental seems to have reached its limit. In the natural sciences we have indeed a huge accumulation of information, but we come to impasses for lack of sufficient insight. In philosophy also, as we shall show, we are coming to the end of our possibilities. And, growing ever more neurasthenic and weaker of will, our time is sinking deeper and deeper into the bondage of death. Ever more rapid becomes the rate of change. Innovations which not long ago were scarcely mastered within generations grow out of date now in a few years. In art, in thought and in the deepest foundations of life, fashions follow upon each other in feverish haste. This is the noon-tide terror. This extreme need, more solemn and more menacing than ever before, proclaims to him who has eyes and ears that all things worldly have now become too narrow, that we are visualizing a breakthrough to higher realms. That which oppressed us we shall now do in freedom not in aversion, but in the all-embracing fervor of love. Now that everything is exhausted we will do the one thing which is new and renews everything: we will rise out of the temporal, which shuts out each from himself, into the God-likeness which includes all within itself.

Passing Through the World Zenith

What terror is more awesome than the noon-tide terror? All around resounds a noise as of rushing enemies—sharp as a scythe and resembling a battle. Fever burns, breathing stops, and overwhelmed with exhaustion we close our weary eyes. Then the spirit of the noon-tide whispers to us its deadly lore. Noon-tide terror enshrouds the world.

But woe to him who condemns the noon-tide terror, who wishes himself back in the morning! He will pine away with longing in the burning noon, for he who shrinks from the evening will not live to see the coming day. And he who cannot bear to undergo the autumn-withering of the world, who is not broken like ripe fruit, as the world is broken, he cannot be born again in the spring-time. The world is ending irretrievably. Ending not in annihilation, but like seed that perishes in order to become forests. There are no more worse prophets today than those who preach what is dead. They start a thousand mummies walking among us and thus hinder the coming of the new glory. They do not say: "What does it matter— let the world go—another glory lights us on, where world is as the seed-particle to its forests."

We have seen the greatest sorrow of all sorrow, the exhaustion of our time, and we know that there is no healing, neither through yesterday nor through a prolonged today, because in these terms there will be no healing at all. And yet there is nothing to complain about or to accuse. This extreme suffering is because "world" has passed its

highest point, has become ripe. And this is as little evil or bad as the
falling of the fruit in the fading autumn.

This is our answer to the problems of our time: *world-at-merid-
ian—then world-descent*. No complaining, only exultation; for a
splendor of extreme joy will begin. *There never was a more overwhelmingly potent time than ours*. Not Rome, nor Jerusalem, nor
the Pharaohs, nor Byzantium, nor any doom-laden hour in history
saw what we are destined to see. We should be overcome by happiness, for when ever before did the confines of the world burst?
Shall we not, then, silence the fear which tells us how insignificant
is our time? What is insignificant is only the wisdom of the swamp;
"hygiene," "reforms," "comfort" and "fads and cults." But never
stood the human before a greater turning-point. Once this is known
in all its depth and fulness, ten thousand trusty vassals of the Eternal will rise up among us and lead the way to the portals of the world.

What after all are we in this rising, falling world? And can
"world" then rise and fall? Is "world" not the great primeval ONE,
the container that includes everything in itself, the sum-total
wherein everything is encompassed? Is it not the All-Mother Nature,
the pitiless mechanism in which we are the tiniest little wheel which
can fail without causing any real trouble? To all this we say, "NO."
We will frighten away the terror and say: "We are no grain of dust
which can be crushed in this infernal machine. NO! Without us, the
All would sink into nothingness. And nothing exists which could
extinguish us".

This is the final wisdom of today: everything is relative, all things
are interrelated with one another. And so "world" too dwindles into
an illusion, and we are thrown back on ourselves. Let us investigate.
What strikes us first is that the lower we descend in the scale of living beings the more the rigidity of the world-picture increases to an
emotionless stiffness, until in the animal there is only the passing
moment. Here the world-consciousness disappears and yields to the
mere experience of the environment, till finally in the plant and the
lowest living beings it becomes complete absorption in the moment.
Experience of the environment is incapable of advancing to the All,
and the more world-enclosed is a being the less it has a world. But
now let us look upwards. Why is it more difficult to look upwards

than downwards? Because *below* us is only our own experience, but that which is *above* us has to be lived in godlike fulness. The world which walls us in will be beneath us. All rigidity then disappears; phenomena acquire a more fluid character; everything solid becomes "the veil of Maya"; and with ever-growing power arises the staggering doctrine of the world as appearance.

Is this doctrine of "world-illusion" conclusive and necessary? No, it is not. It rests on the hypothesis of the world-zenith, otherwise it is not binding. Now that we have lived through it "world" begins to sink beneath us. There is not *one* world and *one* doctrine which is the "right" doctrine, the exact reflection of the "one world," which, out of all the hubbub of opinions will arise some day—or perhaps never. The world must go out of being as it came into being, and which view of it is the "right" one depends on where we stand in its course. The critical consideration of the world surrounding us, the great dis-union between appearance and reality and finally the very consciousness of the "world," *all this could only arise in the course of the world.* Beneath us lies nature's realm, ending in an abyss, but above us and the world lie the Godhead's transcendental boundless realms of abundance.

Is this itself any more than a mere "world-concept", a mental appurtenance of reality? Never! This world-concept is the crowning, the omniscience, the ripening fruit, which we may not harvest till the decline of the world. From being crushed by the world, we ascend, till, in place of the experience of mere environment, world-consciousness enters like the sun. Now that we have experienced "world" up to its zenith and have come forth out of it what we say is no longer only "knowledge" but the expression of the world in all its fulness.

The philosophic cognizance of mankind has always been in step with this growth. It is by no means a meaningless chaos of opinions, as the dogmatism of the so-called exact sciences would make it out to be. Certainly each thinker does his own work, but only as the artist in the orchestra plays his own instrument, and yet all together make perfect harmony. So too is the unanimity of the song of those who contemplate the world.

It is true, however, that in the exact sciences there has never been an opinion that was not subsequently revoked nor a single scientific law which has proved immutable. In the spiritual history of philosophy on the other hand we see, not conflicting directions, but only two which explain everything. The one, a flood of ascending God-like harmony; the other the swamp-wisdom of materialism which drags downwards. In the realm of animal life, materialism may be the purest truth. Today for us it is nothing more than a painful spur. Critical opinion, especially epistemological theory has from of old, taught one thing, quite in accord with our existence and growth in the world and up out of the world: that all reality and all environment are appearance, while we ourselves are the key to the All. In the past such a view was revolution, liberation, a high and holy mission. But we must strongly oppose this doctrine when it attempts to deal in metaphysics. Nothing is worse than metaphysics built up on epistemology. Reflective philosophizing has served no further than to base all riddles on the greatest riddle: ourselves. Now we hover between two abysses: the abyss beneath bristling with death and the God-abyss above.

Let us follow to the end this liberating liberation. What common sense, with its gloomy bias, takes for the only real, is by no means the real. What is it that really acts? That which common sense never sees, the mysterium. We know from of old that the more passionately we try to lay hold on reality, the more it slips from our hands. How it changes, this our self, and draws into a whirl every phenomenon that would rest on it. At one time, silent solitude; at another, the mad rush of a city. A moment ago, filled with awe by the sounds of music, now, already half-asleep, a few pitiful touch-sensations. Now, the eye drunk in a vast expanse of lake and mountains; and again now, the faintest memory. Every pulsation of the soul makes reality dance like a boat in a storm. And deceptive appearance shrouds everything in its mist.

What were hardness without our sense of touch? What were light and color without the eye? But, ask further, *what were our eye without us?* What were sound without the ear? But what the ear without us? And what space and what time in all their infinity without us, for they contain not us but we them. And the eternal laws of mathematics, are they alone conclusive? They depend on us. On the organization of our mind rests our mathematics as logical structure. Scientists have already begun to construct mathematics with a higher number of dimensions as substructure, each of which is just as logical as ours. Should the space-view of our mind alter into one of those modifications, not one stone of all our world would remain upon another.

Equally fluctuating are also cause and effect, singularity and multiplicity, being, and the functions of our mind. Let us go still further and ask: "Are" the categories? "Is" being? The questions are no joke; they are truly apocalyptic. Being cannot overlap itself—it cannot say "I am." It takes flight from itself—it rests on abysses. Something higher encompasses being, a super-being. And if everything is based on knowing, whereon is knowing based? Again on knowing? We never get to the end. *Yet everything indicates that there is something higher and deeper, in which it rests. And this is the secret and the meaning of the human being that he breaks the bounds of the natural and turns depths into heights.*

With our growth in the world and the fundamental knowledge that goes with it, the driving whirl of phenomena sinks ever deeper into the self, but does not come to nothing. It is embedded in the self, which rests on the abyss like a slumbering seed-particle. Being, which today is *in* me, is there *around* me. If we find in the world a "subject-object-process," we find there inversely an "object-subject-process." Let us observe now how in this process "it I's" and how "it thing's," while there is after all but one single course of events.

There is one single process, as sphere-surface and sphere-space are *one* and not *two*. For if I posit sphere-surface, then it encloses the sphere-space. Thus I and the thing in the subject-object act are completely interfused, so that the process all "I's" and all "thing's." This inter-weaving is also quite obvious if the whole process is seen as content and form. At first we are inclined to say: "thing" is content, "I" is form. Presently however we must realize that "thing" is also that which stamps form, and "I" is that whereby "thing" becomes content. Even this duality of the interweaving is again interwoven each with the other, and so on *ad infinitum*. As a symbolic sign of this we choose the letter "X," and we call this view "chiliastic," for it truly is the way things are looked at today. Only the thousand-year view can see that *each single thing stands in totality, and totality rests in each single thing.*

What did we gain when the reality of the world vanished for us? Only that "world" means nothing else now than "MAN." We ourselves become the mystic key and win our manhood. For we forsook everything that lay irretrievably behind us; we left in tears, not in anger. Then the rigid mechanism vanished, this death-dealing machine, which almost annihilated us. Then we feared no more the great "Enlightener" who may any day come forward to tell us that the world is filth, the worst imaginable. Let him tell us. We know better. *The most joyful tidings are that we can burst the framework of the world, and that it falls to us to shape it into highest holiness.*

We have attained to manhood. This is the meaning of the present day. From being ourselves soft clay we have become sculptors of the world. Today we should enter upon our everlasting mission of fashioning the world. At last there opens before us a way into vast new realms, joyous release from the dead world, the purposeless mechanism, born of blind chance. The world is not a mosaic of any sort of physical particles, force-particles or monads. Neither it is ruled by the law of cause and effect. "World" is the seven times holy of holies, the mystery. It is the veil before paradise, a workshop, a purgatory, our mirror, our development, the satellite of God.

Now that we are going forth out of the world, we nevertheless do not wish to flee from the world, for it is God's school and absolutely and entirely divine service. Only today the Father rests, the creation has been completed, and we start on our journeying in the valley. Since the world will fade into world-rest, we must seek a point above the world where we may take it off its hinges, for we ourselves are the primeval cause of worlds. Let us expect no more help from without. We have snapped the umbilical cord, which gave us strength from the depth of creation. After the noon-tide of the world there remains only the working out and fulfilment of the world. This is the bitter anguish of our time, that it is remote from God, utterly forsaken and shut in. There are no loopholes of escape and no deliverance or healing, save only in the divine rebuilding of the world.

What right do we have to speak thus? What kind of condition is it which is less than world, and where is that which overcomes the world? Do we wish to revive the childlike realms of the Kingdom of Heaven? How can we show that, besides what is given as fact, something else "is"? It is the narrowness of our position in the world that we cannot in one stroke make this plain. We must proceed step by step and longingly try to clothe every word with universality. Above every word there will ring the solemn-joyful sound of bells, till amidst them the solitary anchorite's bell sounds louder and louder, and everything in the world soars up with its sound.

By what means shall we penetrate into the heights and depths? By science? Professional opinion knows no other way. We will not take that way, for today we must forget how to crawl. With more daring means and yet with absolute certainty we will attain to our eternal kingdom. Adhering to this bold doctrine, we shall not shrink from the passage of arms with science. Nay, more; to the factual wisdom of science we shall give full credit, such as it can only dream of.

We will grant that nothing ever "is" but what science can include in its grasp; no height and no depth "is" which we cannot touch or catch in the mirror of cognition. This is the very thing to learn—is it not?—to reach something *beyond* what we can touch and not to content ourselves with mere mirroring. We want really to reach our divine home through an unheard-of growth, through the parturient power of the new birth in us, whereof we shall perish like the grain of seed that becomes a flower. We are not to linger in the realm of touch, nor to mirror what is afar off, but to stand sponsors to the deed. Willingly we leave to science that which is the deepest root of its being; but as for us we have no desire to learn swimming on the land. We must manifest that metaphysical courage for the transcendental which we have lost today, clinging as we do solely to the tangible. Now is revealed to us the great mystery: *"credo ut intelligam,"* *"Before I know, I must believe."* What do we know of the cultivation of belief when we have practiced nothing more than the cultivation of knowledge! Is not faith a mere childish "thinking it's true"? The truth is however that not the tiniest bit of knowledge can come into being until a firm standing-ground has been taken up from which this knowledge may be gained. There is not the least bit of knowledge in the world that has not rested on the sure foundation of a belief. It is vain self-deception not to see this; but also an enormous weakness. This is readily understood when another mystery is revealed to us: *"credo quia absurdum," "I believe because it is impossible,"* which means that we have some power over impossibilities. Belief is the super-natural power, which overcomes all contradictions. "If one would say to this mountain: Be removed, and would believe it possible, then the mountain would plunge into the sea". This is more than there is in touch and taste, more than mere mirroring. This is belief that is stronger than "world" and "nature," and places us where in a flash dazzling knowledge is ours. For exaltation is everything. This we must realize as the only way to know how height and depth loom forth into our reality.

We must try, first of all, to penetrate into the Supreme, for there is a law that the higher precedes what is lower and sets it in motion. The Supreme is *a priori* to everything, as in the mosaic the picture guides and directs the design of the whole. It has no existence apart from the picture.

If we wish illumination it is futile to lay hold of what is around us and beneath us on the plane of feeding and feeling. We have to expand in sidereal birth. The higher realm however—we call it gnostically the Pleroma—never means the denial of the lower realm. In seraphic fire it lifts up these lower realms into itself.

The Nature-realm is the depth below, the World in the middle and the Pleroma above, these three form an eternal cycle. They are three members brought into unity in a single organism, like legs, trunk and head. The feet are quite subordinate to the body, which can dispense with them and yet live. Feet and trunk are subordinate to the head. The realm of Nature beneath us is the feet which stand and carry, and the limbs which grasp and hold. The World is the trunk with its circulation, its heart, respiration, nutrition and propagation. The Pleroma is the head which sees and gives guidance and life to the whole. These are three quite different principles. With the *thousand-year-view* we detect in the limbs the life of the body, and in the body the head. Thus the Pleroma does not make a third with Nature and World, but a higher which absorbs both into itself, so that in it they awaken to their own essential being, as limbs and trunk attain their true life only through the head.

The World can only be born in *spirituality*. It is still half-overpowered by Nature, by the depths, and yet drawn into the heights. The Pleroma rests on this: *Above World. Above Nature. Above the corporeal.*

What now is corporeality? The materialist thinks it to be the sum total of all that is real, the only thing that is sure and solid, the only thing that *is*. But that which is all body is dead, completely subdued and has no freedom. Death and limitation, pressure and impact, this is the nature of body. Strife and soaring—this is the nature of World. Creativity, splendor, seraphic glow and eternity—this is Pleroma.

As we gradually awake from the slumber of animalism, corporeality loses its seemingly self-evident reality, and as body is seen as the lower limit of the whole; it loses its independence. That which to ordinary understanding appears to be the sole reality, the only solid thing, crumbles to nil—it is a boundary, the boundary of nothing.

The question may be asked: "Is this free spirituality above the body possible?" Can mind exist without body? We must go deeper than that—we want to know something of the relationship between what is called mind and what is called body. Mind in body can be more glorious than mind without body. A sculptor needs his stone, but he fashions it as the master of it.

The doctrine of "mind without body is impossible," is sacrilege if we take it to mean that mind is eternally fettered to the body. For it is our joy to realize that we are not forever banished to the dungeon of corporeality; we are masters over the temporal and of that which can decay. Mind can exist with body in three ways: as a seed in winter soil sleeping encased in matter, as awakening to sprout forth and struggle with clods of soil and as fashioning matter and forming body. Even in this latter case the body is a dependence, and yet is highest freedom.

Should we now refute the grotesque notion that thinking is a process of the brain, or a mysterious appendage of the body? No! This *is* the ordinary, the general point of view. Those who oppose it are very few, because life today still rests on Nature and is scarcely even World. If everyday life were to raise itself just the least little bit above materialism, this would be an unparalleled revolution and equal to the beginning of Pleroma.

We should not be astonished at the domination of the body and the idea of consciousness as a product of the brain, for the mind of most people is indeed still half-asleep. It often is nothing but a painfully exact translation of their bodily processes into the mental. In our blindness we ask: Where is the mind above matter? Where is the Pleroma in travail in the World? The sprouting germ in us still shuns the light and feels only the clods of soil around it. They seem to be reality, but they are only boundaries. We look upon the bits of mosaic and are blind to the whole picture. The parts—stomach, kidney, lungs and so on—only live because they are together in the unit Man; alone they could not exist at all. We must now clearly experience this impalpable totality—Man. He is a great deal more than the sum of his organs. And is not this wonder of wonders—that all things are meant for him and for one another, that harmony unites all things in love—is not this more than any idea of force-and-matter particles?

We lack as yet a clear experience of that which can be regarded as living reality—this regulator which combines, directs and blends. But even in the most ordinary every-day life it is not the palpable but the super-palpable that is effective, especially in higher organisms. Materialism is the dullest blindness. Can we possibly believe that the body is myself—this body, which as soon as I leave it becomes putrid decomposition? Can we not learn the higher language? In Pleroma we come to live our life and save ourselves from death. But we have a long way to travel.

Nothing in the world retains its life that does not become a stone for building up the Pleroma. As our body eliminates everything that cannot serve for building, so everything that is not capable for becoming Pleroma is rejected and thrust out by the door of death. It sinks back into the nature-abyss till again it is lovingly awakened to begin this journeying anew, until in purity it attains its goal.

We have seen that Pleroma is above the material and yet contains it, that the mechanical changes into the dynamic, and stress and strain into seraphic love. Now we shall see how the common law can become a cosmic law and the individual thing a mere point of departure. Even the simplest, most every-day occurrences remain incomprehensible unless in concrete exaltation we raise each and every one of them and ourselves into the Pleroma. Thus every single thing—out of its isolation—becomes the point of passage of a limitless process. The subjective rises resplendent as the universal law of the world.

"The past cannot be altered." But as soon as anything rises into Pleroma, it attains omnipresence. What had been withdrawn from the sphere of action in the world and seemed to be relegated to an intangible past, in Pleroma is resuscitated, appraised and judged. If there is in it any imperfection, sorrow or regret, it is sent once more through the cycle. Thus, after all, the past *is* altered. The future is the rock on which the past rests.

In the Pleroma, sunshine and fire become seraphic love. The hub of the world is not mechanical materiality, for life and everything else revolves around values. Man is as yet but a grain of sand, compared with the untrodden paths of his possibilities. As in pure oxygen a spark flares up, so in the higher, vital air of the Pleroma the human spark bursts into flame. To live and to rise are one and the same, and the idea of living without rising is a materialistic abstraction. Individual, race, epoch, nation—none can remain *in itself* without falling into decay. *But we need awakened eyes* to look upwards. The worm crawling on the gound knows nothing of the cathedral above it, its spires, its style, the blueprint of the architect or the worship within it.

Are the invisible realms really so invisible? No! They are the most visible of all! The more our senses remain sensual the more dull and animal-like they are. Only supra-animal sense perceives the vernal lustre on the trees, the interrelation of human beings, the upward tendency in everything and that "everything is full of gods." To the enlightened sense the tangible animal-basis dwindles to an abstraction originating in the lower animal understanding. In the transfiguring of actuality we perceive the invisible.

The fundamental experience acquired by the infant is one common to all human beings, to the most intelligent and the most imbecile. The experience of growing is an experience without parallel.

We realize that *"we are greater than the world."* The world-power is not above us nor around us; it is *in* us. And on this fundamental experience and realization rests our hope that life can be divinely revolutionized and re-formed. But at the same time we have to understand that our highest triumph signifies our end, for what must happen is that from slumbering seed comes growing life.

The Pleroma is built from the world as a picture is the resultant splendor of a book of sketches; none need be rejected, every one can be turned to good account. Yet we cannot draw Pleroma out of ourselves, as a spider does its thread. We must rise into it, we must become the new *man*, realizing that world is based on something outside and higher than itself. "World" is not infinite; it borders on Pleroma and has its limits there.

Our present time is the beginning of a new world-epoch. For now World rises into Pleroma, into the holy realm of love. In Pleroma there cannot be division, the ferocious and the tame are not fighting each other, the storm does not break the flower, though both storm and flower exist there. Here in the world, one thing excludes another. There, in Pleroma, all things are interfused in seraphic love with one another, but each in its unique individuality.

The reality of our understanding must show itself in action, not in detached and theoretical "looking on". Here we differ from almost every previous religious consciousness; for we do not flee from the world. The field of our labors is a comprehension and a re-fashioning of the world with a joyous acceptance of it. There can be no Pleroma without the World. All that is above must be discovered here below, for it is indeed here, clad in the raiment of the world. All this seems inevitably to presuppose the existence of that to which as yet we are striving only. But this is characteristic of the world: it must rise beyond itself, must become more than it is at present, must express itself in an ecstasy higher than itself.

When the body is made a unity by the head, the tendency is increasingly outward beyond that of the bodily life alone, so that the head expresses in itself more than its differentiated function as part of a body. If we look at the circulatory system in parts—say, from heart to lungs, or from breath to blood—we cannot understand these parts by themselves, but only in conjunction with the circulation as a whole. The circulation from heart to man is *man*, from stomach to kidneys *man* and from breath to blood *man*, and it is only when on the higher human plane all this is interfused in order to have these organs and processes functioning. Yet, in the superficial prejudices of today, to stare at the isolated part without conceiving it in its relation to the whole, is taken to be exact investigation.

Just as the organs are absorbed in the higher unit *Man*, so Nature, World and Pleroma are absorbed in a higher Whole, in which they are unified. And this Whole is not the sum of the three, but the higher, the Godhead, and this alone, when it is attained, constitutes what in each of them is "reality."

The beginning of sidereal birth is to experience *wholeness* here in this world, not simply as an idea, but as something to be embraced, for the realm of *wholeness* rests in divine transcendence above all formative existence. And just as the relations of our organs are comprehensible only as seen from the "watchtower" Man, so can we understand the inner relationship of Nature to World and World to Pleroma only from the basis of sidereal birth. Then we shall behold wonders: how the ego sets itself free and returns homeward; how the law of Nature signifies the *taking of shape*; the law of the World, *communion*; and the law of Pleroma, *freedom*. Seeing all this but not having experienced the new birth, we may remain *within* the circulation and still undergo the suffering of perpetual recurrence, where everything is mercilessly driven round and round. Did we but remain within, we would fall into madness, yet in the new birth eternal splendor is revealed to us, because the meaning of the circulation is not only return but exaltation.

Now we have taken a step upwards, even higher than the Pleroma, for even Pleroma is a formed realm. It is higher in form and higher in content, form and content infinitely interwoven, super-existent and brought into being by sidereal birth. Yet it is not above all form because it is only the completion of that which had its root in Nature and has been developed in World. Its transcendental capacity cannot contain more than what it has passed through in the eternal circulation of Nature, World and Pleroma, where everything is seraphically in oneness, we reach the place where sidereal birth is completed in the Godhead.

Is then this realm only a petty monistic mixture, in which all richness and color become a grey uniformity? No! Because to stand above form and fulness does not mean to have no fulness and no form, but to have highest fulness and all form in higher unity, a unity pervading all.

This new state demands fearlessness, for it leads out into the open, into an atmosphere which requires a new mode of life. If form existed we would have to experience it, and that would mean we were still *within* the circulation. So there can be nothing which is not ourselves, for we must have lived through all forms. That would mean to experience voluntarily *everything*; that in the new life all may be included.

The meaning of part and form is this: "Only once, and this alone; one single thing without its like." But Godhead is not this form or that, not even the sum-total of form, *but blissful foundation* of all.

Nature, World and Pleroma unite to form a ring, the ring on the hand of God. Nature, with its subjection to forms, and Pleroma with its freedom from them, both point to this hand and both point beyond it—just as subjection and freedom produce the present, where future and past melt. Yet, all that ever came to the life of form will not forever cleave to the dust of finite matter. The forms even will be freed from their finiteness and become boundless and embedded in super-existence.

The ego-form is the highest of all forms and the completion of all forming. It is the place where forming comes to an end, the place of the liberation of all forms. What was below it becomes in the ego a standard and an ideal form. Spirituality takes the place of things; things, symbolic and exalted, are transformed into souls. The ego is on the one hand the supreme development and crown of all forms, but at the same time the pregnant womb in which the super-formed can come to sidereal birth. The ego is in the innermost depths of the circulation as a grain of seed is flower in narrowest confinement. And yet again it is the sacred place in which alone sidereal birth can begin, where the mad whirl of forms can emerge from the circulation and soar to the sunlight of super-existence. This double nature of the ego and its higher spheres we have yet to show in detail.

The ego, when it has stopped circulating stands above the circulation and appears in the fulness of its seraphic content before God— *in the realm where, instead of the existence-function, the transcendental existence-outside-oneself is the norm.* God, then, is above all forms, but He is not a rigid, static perfection. He is the love-glowing at-oneness of all. *He is the transcendental life of all forms*—the beginning and the end, which drives all forms from mechanical subjection to free, absolute creating. "Existence" gives place to a higher form of life of which it has been only a first reflection in the depths. A mind patterned to images cannot see this. It begins to be seen only when the ego attains its higher nature, and in sidereal birth lives without limits in the hovering and soaring of extreme bliss.

We started with the death of the world from noon-tide exhaustion, for the zenith has been reached, and the new, the higher must emerge. The nature-realm is that which the world has passed through, while the heaven-realm is that to which the world is moving. Nature, World and Pleroma seraphically united, are but a single heart-beat, systole and diastole of God.

We shall never rise above circulating if we desire nothing but completion. The realm of completion must include the sphere of the abyss and that of becoming. The sidereally-born craves with equal ardor chaos and abyss and the world. He has no preference, because to the Godhead none is dispensable.

From the blissful heights a valley full of immeasurable horror still separates us, and at this very time we are journeying in this valley. In the death-like sultriness of the world-noon we scarcely notice the faint rustling of the approach of evening, or indeed, of the twilight of the world. And though it seems as if the noon-tide life is pulsating at its fiercest, from the watch-tower of the divine life it is only the remoteness from God of this turning-point, where the swinging pendulum seems to halt for a moment at this lowest point—deepest silence.

Below us is completely crushed, materially stiffened spirit; we ourselves are objective spirit; above us dwells pure spirit. The transcendent glory will come upon us; we shall ascend to an unheard-of new, which alone can break the curse of the noon-tide terror.

We cannot solve the great eternal riddles in the world, the great fundamental questions which are as old as world and man, as long

as we stand on the basis "world." Even if we refine observation and
investigation to the utmost, we will not be any nearer to the solution.
These riddles are tensions as necessary within the world as digestion
and breathing to the body, and their unravelling can only come when
in sidereal birth we rise out of the world-abyss. We shall never be able
to grasp "truth" as the fruit of *worldly* effort. In order to see we must
advance to the unclouded vision that cannot descend to us, as the
ocean cannot enter into the drop.

The blissful primeval rhythm has no place in the world; there,
where material law and worldly existence must rule, it would suffocate. The seraphic space of Godhead is its place. *The most holy divine life must not be fettered by its organs.* There is a hallowed law
of rotation in the circulation—in the *direction* of a life higher than
that of the circulation alone.

What we have here set forth seems now ripe to be justified before the forum of science. Our future life will never be satisfied with
science as a basis. We shall rise above science to an infinitely richer,
clearer light. Nevertheless we must acknowledge that when the scientific spirit took possession of mankind, it was one of the most important events in history. Science drove the human being out of his
childlike innocence and matured him into man. Man, as an individual cannot become young again, except in his children, so the human
race can only rejuvenate itself in new birth beyond itself. An impulse
towards objectivity took possession of us, and it is good that it has
happened. This scientific awakening has freed our spirit from the op-
pression of the world, till the last fetter and the last idol are falling
from us.

Yet philosophical investigation has not been able to find the
standard of truth—Jesus was silent when Pilate asked the eternal question—because in the terms of this world the question cannot be answered. The sciences have now taken the place of the philosophies.
First, philosophy was thrust by theology into the dogmatic fetters of
the old tyrannical God; then, natural science sought to exalt the
lower nature-realm above us and to merge everything in physics. Now
national-economy and psychology put forward these lower regions
of human existence as a substitute for philosophy. On the other hand,
in philosophy itself we clearly note two directions. The one, positive,

metaphysical, of which we have already said that with varying complexion it is yet one single rising flood of harmony; the other, the theory of cognition which, like Mephistopheles, is always rousing us again and asking: "What is Truth?"

This illuminating theory of cognition has passed its zenith in Immanuel Kant. It is no mere chance that his emergence coincided with the victory of the bourgeoisie in the French Revolution, developing the materialistic reasoning to its highest potential. The present book stands at the close of this epoch and at the beginning of the new age where the noon-tide drowsiness is about to pass off behind the world-summit, where world is just beginning to decline, and a higher world is making itself known.

Kant—this is the dramatic zenith, but at the same time the start of the dethronement of traditional philosophizing. We know of no greater Kant reverence than the *setting-up of the great Anti-Kant*, for we had more than enough of those, for whom Kant is the "Old Chinese." It is a sign of extraordinary spiritual narrowness to label a great man as either an idol or a destroyer, instead of administering in free creative abandon the legacy he has bequeathed to us.

Without Kant we would still be quite choked up with the object, with the material, fettered to the presumably solid ground of experience. Kant has destroyed forever this lower kind of metaphysics. He has, Copernicus-like, wrenched experience out of its firm position as a resting-point, making it revolve round the sun of our mind. But this great liberator was not great in formative power. Where Kant wished to build up the positive, he found no other means than those he had himself disparaged as inadequate. He did not get beyond the bodily conditioned intelligence, whose kingdom is so entirely of this world. He did not achieve a synthesis. *Liberation* is his achievement, and *freedom* is the great basic strength of the *Critique of Practical Reason*. Not yet, indeed, that limitless divine transcendental freedom, but—as it were—a citizen's legalized freedom. Yet this is still one of the loftiest ideas of all times. The *Critique of Practical Reason* is the key to all of Kant's work, the utmost motive of all his efforts, and without it the *Critique of Pure Reason* is quite incomprehensible.

The theory of cognition is eternally great because it has forever taken objectivity off its hinges. It has dissipated reality, dethroned the absolute, and brought all fact to an end in relativity and phenomenalism. The more the theory of cognition established thinking as self-governing, the more it forced us to the boundary of thinking, where there is no possibility of halting but only of going beyond. The revolutionary solution was in no sense constructive. There can be no greater error than metaphysics built upon the theory of cognition, for it could not advance a hair's breadth beyond the *facts*. It is precisely the crassest empiricism, and complete immanence is its essence.

If we wish to gain an understanding of the spirit of science, then the theory of cognition stands at the entrance to the higher realms because it is the science of *knowing*. But just as dogmatic theology, or natural science, psychology or economy cannot be the foundation of higher knowledge, so too we cannot build on the theory of cognition, for it exists only within the narrowest limits of the world. Above and below the world it has no validity. It is never free from hypothesis: it is rather "World" alone and that is its hypothesis. It starts from the subject that knows and the object that is known. What is to be known must first enter into cognition, if knowing is to be the result. How this mirroring takes place, whether indeed it is possible, this is precisely the field of the theory of cognition. But all these hypotheses and questions are purely of this world.

"World" is the labile state of equilibrium, this strife of subject and object, where complete subjection to matter is indeed past, but divine transcendence and full freedom have yet to be acquired. World is that condition of tension between the depths of *nature* and the Pleroma-realm of fulness and completion, which points beyond itself to the realm of divine One-ness.

Philosophers of a materialistic and retrograde tendency have resolved everything into the objective, and in these objectivized realms the ego shrank to a mysterious center-point. Other philosophers of a forward tendency have turned all data more and more into something subjective, until the object vanished into the extreme conception of the "thing in itself". Subject and object are not, however, halves which join together to form a whole, but they are points of view. Looking backwards, everything condenses into object; looking forwards, everything dissolves into subjects. *If I objectivize,* I approach the material mechanical death-abyss, and hence everything, even the spiritual resolves itself into logical forces, as with Hegel. *If I turn to the subjective,* everything becomes alive and finally ends in the vitality of the self.

What is objectivity? If we conceive it to be constraint, we have already set it in relation to the subjective; already we have lost the unattached objectivity resting in itself. However we never can arrive at pure objectivity, for that would be equivalent to death. Kant's inclination is always directed towards the thing. Such cognitions cleave anxiously to the death-realm of things as the sole reality, and strive after the "thing-in-itself" as the innermost secret, whereas we wish to rise *out of* the realm of things to solve the riddle. The goal of the self-reliant ego is the wisdom of all those who do not wish to lay down their ego, who wish to have experience without stirring themselves, who want the view from the summit but remain at the foot of the mountain. We cannot admit that Kant exalted the self, since for him too, at least in the *Critique of Reason* it is only a mirror which receives the equally lifeless raw-material. "Object" is nothing but a certain way of living, a cognition oriented by death, and "thing" is but an early stage when life has not yet been lived. In those regions the unawakened self lives only in the mechanical things that have not yet passed through the fire of the personal. It is the capitalistic idea of enrichment through *having and accumulating* instead of through *growing*. The "in-itself" motif does not penetrate into the heights and depths but leads to a reversed metaphysics, trying to view phenomena from behind.

To us the constraint of the objective never appears as a thing but as an order. Why must I always see this star there, why always this same forest? Why on awakening do I always find my room as before? Why all these people see the same play on the stage? Is there really a star, a forest, a scene which we reflect or absorb? First of all, we know nothing but that all sorts of sense-impressions, feelings, efforts, thoughts are ordering themselves into a whole which we call star, forest, stage. Yet it would be premature to conclude that all this is *my* imagination, for it is still a question whence comes this order, which has fitted these raw-materials together to make forest and star? Or again. Who has ever *seen* that hydrogen and oxygen combine to make water? No one, and no one will ever see it. We see only that there is a quite definite arrangement in what we observe: color-impressions, heat-sensations, noises, smells and other structural elements of consciousness arrange themselves in definite space and time as a picture. But whence comes this arrangement?

The thing-ward directed theories point to the conception of the "thing-in-itself" causing the compulsory arrangements. The theories directed upward speak of the logical mechanism of the categories in the ego. *But neither of the two will explain to us why we hear the trees rustle in the wood and see the stars sparkle.* That feelings and thoughts, efforts and sensations arrange themselves to form these things, to constitute just this detail and this objective constraint, *this is not any kind of mechanism. This is a resplendent practical growing vitality, goal and mission, an urge toward loftiness and divinity, but no more mechanical than the ordered setting out of the colors on the palette for the masterpiece.* This fundamental tone of objectivity, this rigidity, this mute constraint is full of sacred awe, tidings from on high and an urgent challenge. The "thing-in-self" is but the dry bones of the objective and its death-limit.

But, grown to manhood, we want to alter the world, not merely look at it. If everything possible has happened before, sidereal birth has not happened yet!

The most objective of all is the absolutely single thing. The more we move away from the separated towards the inter-related, the more everything is saturated with the ego. Now what is the single, what is the thing? We reply: There is no single nor any "thing." The material points to the whole, is interwoven with the *All, is* the All. Ever more and more must we have recourse to the *All* in order to understand the most minute thing. Each thing is the whole *All* in this realm of the boundary between the heights and the depth, for it is the mission of each single "thingness" to be a turning-point.

That which has been sent forth out of the divine embrace, robbed of all freedom and has sunk into complete subjection, is now to be set free in order to ascend. The more remote from God, the more unfree, the more stripped of value and significance, the more real is the phenomenon. The narrow border where the kingdom of the depth meets the kingdom of the height, *where depth tries to turn into height, that is objectivity.*

Then everything appears atomistic, cut up into little bits that can never be welded into a unit. As the physicist does not explain how force can be transferred from one to another, so the philosopher does not explain how his bits of the world can mutually influence each other; how subject acts on object, how the will affects thought. But to the supramundane view all these parts and pieces become organs of the whole, transition points and turning points; and subject and object are blended in mutual permeation. We cannot understand the combination of the organs of our body if we do not view them from the higher comprehensive standpoint of circulation and assimilation. Thus, thought and will, subject and object, and all parts of the world will remain separated if we investigate them according to experience. In that endless journeying whose beginning is the unprecedented event of our time, there is coming into the midst of us, into our experience and our action, something that is not merely "world." In place of mechanical action and reaction we have the one all-interwoven life, and there arises multiplicity of the many in genuine community, in Godhead.

There are yet two pairs of opposites that present the completely world-bound basis: the conceptions abstract and concrete, *a priori* and *a posteriori.* These are nothing more than directions of the course of the world, not names for realities but to be understood purely in a dynamic sense. The concrete condenses, but it narrows; the abstract expands but dilutes.

If the professorial expression "system of philosophy" is to have any meaning for us, it can be only this: to unite all existing philosophies in a systematic table, for *there can be no more philosophy.* We know that all "questions" are states of strain resulting from the condition of the world, and *that it is in the nature of every question that it is unanswerable,* since the strain cannot be relaxed through answering, but only through rising out of this world-state. It is impossible finally to form a world-picture, for it is not a something that can be portrayed and that might be hung up in our inner selves. The ever-flowing God-current is not to be copied; the place of the copy is taken by the transcendental impulse within us.

These descriptions of the philosophers are only a combination-game on a large scale. On the side of objectivity: the space-time and mechanical principles, multiplicity, the many-fold kinds of association, unity. On the side of subjectivity: the appreciations of the mind, thinking, feeling, willing. Philosophers used all these fragments, now making one important, now another. All their judgments were genuine and true! None indeed could fully satisfy. They were expressions of actual conditions of life. But today, when with the world all philosophy must end, there remains only the table of all philosophies.

We have been trying to free objectivity from the bonds of materialism, that it should no longer be thing-oriented, and should no longer rotate around death but around the living self. From a thing it should become the God-sent mission and "paragranum" (Paracelsus: "super-seed"). In objectivity or subjectivity alone we cannot find the path to the higher. We must not objectivize the higher, or materialize it, but elevate and liberate the objective.

What now is "Being"? According to Kant it is a category or a capacity of our mind for arranging facts, and indeed the most general and most basic category which nothing escapes. Besides Being there are numerous other categories, but they cannot all with equal justification be ranged side by side in one table. Rather they form an organism of polar character and mediate between the two poles of which one is Being, the other causality and teleology. We find this polar opposition also in the outward-directed powers, space and time. *Space* is the objective lower, a lifeless mechanical thing-comprehending entity, a frozen infinity. *Time*, on the other hand, is the much more comprehensive higher, the more subjective, the quite non-material, dissolved space which points to supra-form. Whereas we can traverse Space in any direction, the direction of Time is determined in one sense. The spatial is tangible, the temporal impalpable. Space is only a differential instance of Time.

In what relation do Space, Time and other categories stand to one another? Space and Time are directed more outwards and serve for representation. We ourselves play a more passive role in them. The categories serve for linking together, which begins externally in Being and rises to causality, to culminate internally in the conception of purpose. In Space there is more extension, but in Time we already have direction and potential purpose, just as in Being we have repose, while in purpose there is motion. In Space and Time, as well as in the categories, there is a constraining mathematical logic, a Logos. *The Logos at rest acts aesthetically, the Logos in motion ethically.* There is a trinity of the logical, ethical and aesthetical. The deepest root of Space and Time lies in aesthetics, the function of understanding in ethics, and the one perpetually wants to turn into the other. With causality and purpose, there is an order of values above the mere linking-together of things. We can now set free all the categories from the substratum of Being and replace the mechanically logical by value-categories.

Hitherto philosophy and science have been seeking an ultimate fundamental principle, a kind of *matter*, whether it be substantial or an objective or subjective metaphysical substratum. All these *matters* have been born from the spirit of *Being*, as species of Being. But we hold that no explanation of the world can be based on any *matter*. It can only be based on the manifestation of God and on the creation-above-Himself. The eternal cycle from Nature to World to Pleroma and the seraphic at-oneness in the divine transcendence is the manner in which we must regard *Being*. *Downwards* it becomes ever more mechanical and ends in death and complete servile subjection; but *upwards* it rises into consciousness. Escaped from the dungeon of Being, it will soar through infinity. No longer can we live shut in by things, nor in the having of things. We want more. We want to grow to all infinities and capacities, destroying narrow confinement in a theoretical mirror-reflection or in getting and having and fattening the ridiculous little ego.

Science has been able to accomplish her great mission to make us grow to manhood, to mature us and to free us from materialism. But as it is itself subjected to material law, it does not avail to lead us a single step towards the divine life.

To early experience everything encountered is still immovably firm, cradled in the certainty of the material. It is the mysterious, the most colossal event in the history of the human being, how this certainty vanishes, how, from being eternally ordained, the world becomes an illusion imposed upon us momentarily for a sacred purpose.

Fact is no longer that which is most certain, it has become the most enigmatic. The world, of all things the most real, is at the same time the most transcendent, for the Here and the Beyond aim to merge. We pass then beyond experience, we transcend. May we then have recourse to the transcendental? Not only may we, not only can we, but we *must*. This is the meaning of all we have been saying. A doubt can only exist as long as we still ask: "*Are* there—outside experience— yet other forms and things; *are* there yet higher regions?"

But super-empirical things have no existence, no more than has the petty pretended transcendence, which seeks with the clutch of perception to reach into the Beyond but which serves only to grasp what has already been experienced. It is not ours to know, but to rise through the superhuman action of belief. The transcendence that we mean is sidereal birth. *Up, out of and above experience*, this is the significance of all that is above the animal; all that is the whole pride and dignity of humanity.

Pure experience which—by the men of exact science prized as invulnerable—is scarcely more than a vegetable-existence; certainly it is not even animal-life. Limited to it, we would remain miserably absorbed in the moment. In that case, could we ever practice exact chemistry? It is already transcendence if we speak of the simple fact of chemical combination, for no such combination is "fact," but primitive facts build themselves up within us in that super-objective arrangement. It is a mistake to believe that our life runs its course in the empirical, in experience. The higher we rise the more everything is saturated with metaphysics. There is no longer anything that rests in itself and does not point outwards. We can live only *above* experience, which serves as a basis, while in so-called pure experience we only vegetate. It is altogether brutish, and cowardly too, to cleave merely to fact. To break through facts is human, human alone.

There is a foolish strife between the camp of empiricism and that of speculation. Fact is sacred, and thinking is sacred. As on the one hand we dethrone reason—for it is a worldly tool and of no service as a guide to the heights—so on the other hand we feel even more strongly that our momentary observations remain stuck in the lower realms. To the open mind, both experience and thinking rest in transcendence. They are neither ways to transcendence nor hindrances;

they are portals into the higher realms. It is just as materialistic to explain the external by the internal as conversely. Subject and object are explained not *by* but *in* each other. The one cannot be asserted over the other, each must balance the other, as the two directions of a proceeding whose unity we experience in the higher manifestation of the Pleroma.

Materialists rather pride themselves on emphasizing the objective conditionality and dependence of the mind, yet *they experience nothing else but this objective mind.* This may be compared to the narrow border where the sea breaks on the shore. Within this limited region the coast-line may well exert an influence which however, further at sea, disappears faster and faster, and very soon completely. The lower, worldly experience and the "exact" investigation of science play their parts exclusively upon this narrow line, where the land of objectivity and of our own lower animalism meets the boundless sea of the mind. Such half-awakened consciousness must rest in the delusion that we are nothing but this body, and that our mind is this body's consciousness.

Today we are advancing beyond the narrow stage where body and mind seek to separate from each other; *we are awakening to the living human spirit.* A vision dawns overpoweringly upon us that we shall slip off the constraint of the body, and that the iron-clad power of death will become a fashioning chisel in our hand. And he who above all theories has experienced how we emerge from matter to exaltation, has forever done with all sombre sobriety and timid distress. We want to face life in fulness. *The general concepts too must become facts of life.* If we not only *think* totality but *live* totality, then the world's base trembles. This is the step into the realm of the higher mind, where that which was before an abstract idea has become the most concrete and has been lived through. And, conversely, that which previously was the most concrete possible, *which was thing,* is resolved into the abstract, becomes a symbol, and becomes the *word* that is with God.

Beyond the material mechanical concepts, abstract and concrete, is enthroned the realm of completion. As we pass through the world-zenith, heaven and earth begin to change into each other. In this way, then, consciousness is elevated to being-alive in the realm of completion, so that we should scarcely call it consciousness any more, rather spirituality. Consciousness is still always conscious "of" something. The lower mentality has not yet awakened to the living divinity of supra-consciousness. The intellect cannot bring forth anything new out of itself.

All wealth and color originating in the worldly workshop of consciousness are, in supra-consciousness, set free from materialism and Being and become God-symbols. Nothing is any longer by itself, everything is seraphically embraced. It is life freed from the clutch of pettiness and limitation, no longer simply Being. That which oppressed us has become our tool. And in completion there the cycle of Nature-depth, World-midst and Pleroma-height is closed.

The Hyacinth Journeying

The ego is the key to the world and world the life of the ego. World is the realm of nature that has risen to subjectivity. All that is separated, thing-like, mechanical, all that is dead only attains to life in the ego; only in the ego are all things interwoven. The ego is the first that has ever been able to exist in some kind of freedom and independence in its own right. *The ego is the causative meaning of all preworld existence: the birth of the world explains nature, as world is explained by the fact that Pleroma is to be born.* But as we rise above the world, and set all its fulness free from the grip of death, so too we shall go forth and above the separate ego to a higher self. As the present world became for us a means of ecstatic, creative soaring, so we shall slip out of the confinement of the little individual ego.

The meaning of the seed is that it must die. To become a seed it had to feed, drawing into itself all fulness, but when it has become ripe and has reached its deepest winter rest, there can follow nothing but development. The culture of the ego becomes madness if it seeks to preserve the dead grain *as it is.* The morality of feeding must be replaced by the morality of sowing. Nothing can be simpler and more self-evident: throw the ego into the fruitful soil of the divine transcendence, and the Pleroma, our higher self, will germinate.

The ego derives its origin from feeding; only by feeding can it grow. The mature ego however can but exist in seraphic self-opening, in germinating. The individual ego cannot rest in itself; it *must always have a task, a mission if it is not to perish.* Up to the present the ego has accomplished an immeasurable task—it has overcome the realm of nature and has carried the formation of the world to the height of our time—so that world has reached its highest state and can grow no more. Therefore, the ego must not let the world sink beneath it and rise. *World dissolution, world-liberation, world-fulfilment, the changing of world into Pleroma, is the task we must undertake today.*

We shall not weary of repeating that liberation can be brought about only by breaking through the world, not by any "doctrine" or "reform" or "technique." Growing beyond world cannot come without destruction of the ego, which will be enforced by deadly necessity if we do not enforce it ourselves. The diminutive ego which we cling to is merely a border-point, the most sacred turning-point and zero-point. When everything rotates around the ego, there, for a while, is world, dominated and fashioned by devouring, that is, by the law of death.

The ego was the growth of the world—but is also destined to set the world free from its rigidity. To be human means to pull oneself by one's own hair out of the swamp. The ego perpetually revolutionizes life and sets values. After the world of feeding and death follows the conquest of the world for God. The human ego is always greater than fact but infinitely smaller than the non-fact seen by God. As the ego comes forth out of the world, it has included within itself the whole universe. Not that *I* live but that I *live* becomes the essential.

Before going further, let us remind ourselves that we make a sharp distinction between the individual and the One. The *individual* is the place of abundance where all diversity originated, the place of the varied development; the *One* contains all abundance in seraphic at-oneness. The individual is basic and indivisible, a zero-point and turning-point. The One is the transcendent and the highest blended vitality of all individuality.

We distinctly wish to avoid the error of all identity doctrines, which abolish abundance in favor of a point of unity. All speech as yet refers to the individual and not to the One; the word now is only

the echo of individuation. The *silent speech* of the all-interfused One
has not yet become possible. Unity and fulness then belong together
like the sphere-surface and sphere-space, and between the two me-
diates the polarity, making one out of two by joining and interfusing
two separatenesses. Polarity is the way of separating and also of fus-
ing together. Not only Nature, World and Pleroma, even Godhead
and the whole cycle rest on the law of polarity. Polarity is the characteristic of the profoundest and ultimate secrets out of which world
arises. It is at once unity and duality.

Thus equipped, let us consider the relation of mass and the individual ego. We must abandon the idea that the ego is simple and
the mass composite; that the ego is the atom and the mass a resultant action of these atoms. The conceptions of the individualistic
West and the more impersonal East are here in sharp opposition.
Mass power and ego power are titanic world-movements, always oc-
curring in combination, neither without the other. A mass can be like
one individual, and in one individual lives the spirit of the mass. Often a mass, be it a people, a calling or a class of society, vibrates in-
stantaneously with one life as if it were a single individual, and in
fact it is indeed a unit. And likewise there lives in everyone the life
of the mass. Only to a crude view does it appear strange that *One*
may now appear manifold and now simple. Unity and diversity are a
polarity—two different points of the same rotation.

In the realm of nature the individual being is lost in the mass,
in the species, the race, the genus. The preservation of the individual
is not important; every care is bestowed on the persistence of the
genus. So completely can the individual be merged in the general
genus that in primitive uni-cellular creatures reproduction coincides
with the end of the individual creature. In the world of the human
ego death rages furiously, making a fearful tragedy of every case. But
only apparently. When in the human being the individual finally becomes a person, at that turning-point the genus vanishes into the
person and the *person expands* into the genus, thus taking on immortality. He rises above the sphere of death, for death rules only
where the individual soul rests in the brief state of wintry frost,
where it is *physical soul, hyle.* This limited person would have to perish, when not fulfilling a supra-personal task, for *it is only the supra-*

personal life, which is not rooted in the physical, that blissfully soars above death.

Until now the supra-personal task was the absorption of nature by the ego and the building-up of the world. *Today it is the conquest of the world in seraphic embrace and the achievement of the Pleroma.* Whereas the ego has been conditioned by the genus, by multitude, by mass, now it must conquer the mass. It can do this only by *becoming itself the genus.* Then can begin that language which is not merely the echo of the individual but the presentiment of the One, that silent speech like the speech of the pious pilgrim who journeyed to St. Francis of Assisi, and after a long silent embrace departed comforted without having uttered a word.

The world-turning-point of our day must necessarily be a time of rationalism, because everything instinctive and intuitive has vanished from among us, and the new intuition is not yet born. A person acts instinctively when the act answers a purpose and the person is not conscious of this purpose. The person is driven by something, he carries out a useful act through a power mightier than himself, and we understand that it is the spirit of the species which is acting through him. The species acts this way also in every creature, be it an animal or even a plant.

Motivation and instinct are indissolubly linked with the supra-personal. The sex-instinct is an expression of the nature-motivation of the still world-crushed individual. The social instinct is but faint in comparison with the violence of the sex-instinct and seems to have a far slighter metaphysical basis. But quite wrongly. *The social is precisely the crown of the supra-personal,* if it is not the herd-instinct but chosen in freedom. The primitive urge of the sexes wants to embrace every Thou without distinction. Yet the true meaning of the sex-instinct is an insistence that ultimately *the one man and the only woman shall unite in fusion.* On the other hand the social instinct strives to free the individual ego from its self-love. The social is an expression of the tendency towards diversity, fulness and unity in the divine cycle; the sexual shows the polarity of the world. It is an eternal law of the world that the polarity of man and woman must make one of two. The creative power of generation and reproduction is based on this creative duality. Thus, through surrender, the woman becomes person and the man loses his personal limitation by hurling himself into the love-abyss.

Reproduction rests on this polarity. It is an expression of the immense disparity of the depth in nature from the world-zenith and the realm of fulness; a disparity that cannot be bridged by the single individual. Countless individual beings are necessary for this, and since the single life in its narrowness must be circumscribed by death, generations by generations must carry on this task. In nature-depth the change of the generations is not much more than repetition; but when the individual becomes less and less part of the "mass", he is able to project the following generation much further above himself. The step from one generation to the next becomes greater, the tempo of the development becomes quicker, the chasm between parents and children deepens. As the steps lengthen, the impulse of the reproductive capacity decreases, the natural life becomes exhausted within us and the desire for children becomes weak.

This weakening of the reproductive power is tragic, because precisely in the highest development of the world, the necessity for the child is the most urgent. Only among lower creatures is the species guaranteed by vast numbers! In world-environment everything is based on the individual child. A people, the "Family of Man," cannot beget a child; the child is the product of the altogether personal. As in the declining world we approach the Pleroma, person widens to the supra-personal, rising above corporeality. The new marriage is consecrated, far above the order of nature. Thus the tragedy of decay at the world-crisis is at the same time the *annunciation of the new marriage exalted above nature and world.*

In spite of the dwindling generative power, the sexual desire flares up with increasing violence—and indeed this inordinate desire is a symptom of decay. *The highest point of the erotic is the lowest of the seraphic.* The erotic is of a differentiated nature, the seraphic of an integral nature; the erotic is limited, the seraphic infinite. The seraphic begins softly, but rises mightily above all isolation. The erotic is a pale reflected splendor of the seraphic, betokening the autumnal and wintry self-enclosure of the self.

Seraphic loving can only increase itself; it is a consuming fire before which the ego flares away. *The erotic can only weaken itself* and ends actually in disgust. *The transformation of the erotic into the seraphic* is one of the great guide-lines. The ever-expanding ego is a joy to which nothing can be compared; it is as if the intoxicating moment of sexual enjoyment had become eternal. The erotic is but the half-blissful, half-shuddering flickering of the body which, perishing, plunges into the bliss of wedded interfusion where isolation ends. In the seraphic the self loses all bonds of narrowness to expand in the limitless embracing of fulness.

When will this great joy triumph over the lesser joy of eroticism? The domination of eroticism can never be broken by asceticism, only by a higher joy. All asceticism is crippling and self-deceptive. There should not be a pre-mature cutting-off of the sex-instinct before the person has passed the world-zenith.

We turn now to the question of property. The contrast resulting from the struggle for property has not only endured through all ages, but has actually increased. It is no accident that this violent discord has reached a dramatic maximum. Property is the touchstone which none can evade. The world-zenith, the remoteness from God, the sealing-up of our infinite self in the dead husk of the person, the passionate intensity of the desire for property—all this is one thing. *Not-having is the way to the Godhead.* The Divine may not possess, for it is overflowing bounty above all materiality and not shutting-up-in-itself. Property makes indolent and separates the one from the other and from the world: *it is the absolute death of the seraphic.* All creative vibration, all blissful journeying is crippled by anxiety about property, which makes a philistine of a human being. A person's desire to possess means binding himself to the zero-point and the end of his world-journeying. The values that have arisen from property are getting exhausted; possessing can no longer act creatively; individual possession loses all claim to life. The proletarian-socialistic movements have not recognized this yet. True socialism desires not the wealth but the holy poverty of the individual, though it does desire the wealth of the community. To this true socialism the proletarian movement is at best a preliminary, and we must not expect too much from it as we must not expect too much from the affluence of the bourgeoisie.

The experiment of reforming society purely by economic methods may be undertaken in the most expert way possible, and with the utmost ingenuity we may harmonize prices, wages, hours of labor and other economic factors—the increasing greed and possessiveness will upset everything. If we do not take this into account and do not succeed in setting a limit to them, then the harmony of all the factors is unattainable. In the past it was not possible to limit personal possessions, but as soon as the advanced position of the proletariat raised the standard of living, it became necessary to demand this limitation. The misery of the masses is not simply a consequence of a wrong economic system; it is brought about by the state of the world and especially by property. A higher morale and a fundamentally new ascent of humanity is not possible on the basis of property. *Only the ending, not the strengthening of property* can lead to this.

A profound expression of a supra-personal, universal connectedness of all individual beings with one another, we find in *India's* doctrine of the transmigration of souls, and of Karma (destiny), which each person builds for himself in life, forming the basis for his next incarnation. According to the *Western* conception, the soul emerges from a mysterious darkness and vanishes into it after a single life. According to the *Indian* conception, every individual passes through numerous lives, whose successions represent a constant purification. Apparently two antipodal worlds! Yet the Indian also presupposes a beginning and a goal, and the Western builds a bridge to the past and to the future by heredity.

The doctrine of repeated existence is not to be interpreted other than as the view that *a common bond embraces all humanity from the beginning,* that we are interrelated with countless others more or less intimately. It means that every fragment of humanity pours itself through the All. It does not mean countless repetitions of a limited ego, but brotherly interfusion. He who has learnt to say "I am not this personal narrowness, mine is the world, all depths of nature and all heights of heaven", he who has learnt this, feels one with all the past and future. The contradiction between the one and only life and the repeated life vanishes if we recognize re-birth as the strongest intensification of brotherliness.

Our body makes us realize our task. It is the strongest expression of our deadly limitation to the territory of this world. We must renounce the materialistic delusion that *the body is an organ of cogni-tion*. It is not adapted for cognition, *it is solely made for action*. Cog-nition is extreme interfusion, divine immediacy. Corporeality on the other hand is intense narrowing. *The organs of the body serve for selection but never for cognition.* Our bodily existence is the turning-point between depths and heights. That which seeks the height must become subjective in Promethean liberating; so for a moment it at-taches itself to our body.

The tension between body and spirit in us is the expression of the great polarity of divine spirit and material spirit. Our body is the organ of our lower limit in sensuousness. Simultaneously it is the highest point of the nature-material. When, on its world-journey-ing from the Godhead, the self has reached the material spirit, then the body indicates to the self that remoteness from God has been at-tained and serves to turn it back. Having risen above world and pos-sessions, above nature and instinct, above consciousness, in order to base all this not on material limitation, but on divine transcendence, *we must, as the most difficult of all steps, forsake our body too.*

We cannot conceive spirit and body as a firmly joined special or-ganism, nor as an empty vessel. Both ideas are determined by a con-ception according to subject and object. They do not do justice to the profound meaning of the ego as an anti-pole of God. The different capacities and activities of the spirit, its thinking, receiving impres-sions—these are not separate functions, they are different directions of a *collective whole*. The spirit is thinking, feeling, willing, *as a whole at the same time*. The transcendental is not mood or feeling (as we might think if we knew nothing of sidereal birth). The trans-cendental merely uses feeling as the yet unformed universal, the opening by which it enters the soul. It comes out again *formed* in the *understanding*. The will is the most primeval essence of the individ-ual, where constraint ever turns to freedom; it is the link between emotion and thought, where the obscure urge to action strives to take form. "I will" means I step forth out of constraint into the midst of the transcendental; I am no longer an animal. Between emotion and thought, between pausing and willing, between sensuousness and spirit, there pulses a never-resting life; the one is ever trying to change into the other; here nothing ever exists alone.

If we consider *memory* we clearly see the impossibility of an individual explanation. Memory is mostly explained as a sort of storehouse. The fact that we possess memory is the tragic expression which denotes that we are separated from the divine all-embracing view of the whole. Memory is the first glimmer of re-awakening, a beginning of renewed seraphic life, and the inclusion of all which lies outside the limitation of the present. It is not the capacity for making a past-present once more present. *Memory is the basis of self-consciousness.* As soon as the ego becomes conscious of itself, its rigidity lessens and ego-liberation begins. But do I know myself? By no means! With my worldly ego, my lower consciousness, I cannot experience my own higher reality.

The ego to which we cling and which is the object of our present-day culture, is but the tiniest part of the self. My whole self in its heights and depths rests in God, although its worldly body pulsates in perpetual renewing. *Only with the inclusion of the Godhead is the self a whole.* To experience one's self means to experience the whole of the divine cycle, it seems to be merged in something greater.

As a violin requires to be played, so the ego requires to expand itself. *There can be no greater absurdity than the ego as its own end. In the whole cycle there is nothing that could be less an end in itself than the human being.* Indeed it is the *divine life* within us that is lifting us above the plane of animal-existence. Only thus are we really living. *Man cannot be his own property without falling prey to death; man cannot be the task of man.* Humanity belongs to Divinity. I am only lent to myself. Not my smallness, but the whole expanse of the world is my supra-personal task. So little is the purely personal its own end that it can only be a divine jest.

The ultimate cause of all decadence is the lack of a supra-personal task. The limited, separate ego is stuck fast in the yet undeveloped germ-condition of the self. However, when *world* has fulfilled itself above its zenith, when the ego has completed itself, then all ego-culture becomes decadence.

For us the great meaning of the world-crisis is that instead of a mechanical unity in the death-point, we must find our unity in divine soaring. The ego seeks death, not the lower death of extinction, which is the eternal fate of the finite, separate self, but the higher

death of transport, which is highest delight. The orgiastic delight of
the body in the transcendence of sensuous contact in sexual pleasure,
is but the physical zero-point of such bliss. For the narrow self is but
a part, and where is a part there is also a counter-part. *The separate
self must hate in order to be.* It is capable of nothing higher than being, and such being rests on the death-manifestation of hate. But the
love-self is no limitation; it is a flowing spring. Its life is no fencing-
off and filling of itself; it is a boundless radiation, a new form of life,
the saving of life in losing it. Not my miserable trembling self, but the
flowing of God through me is the real. My vitality above all death depends solely on the journeying of my smallness to the expanse
of God.

Now that world and all it can ever give is exhausted nearer draws
the moment when we shall forsake the intra-mundane in order to
journey from outlived to new possibilities. We know, from the law of
the deepest way that nothing is forsaken before the last quantum of
value has been lived out of it, and therefore all groaning about human
backwardness, about remaining in the depth, in the animal, about
stubborn unchangeability and baseness, only shows our blindness.
To him who has eyes it is plain *that for leading the world upwards
nothing needed to be better than it was.* The higher self would have
been completely unfitted to elevate *World from Nature.*

Only that higher self which is already beginning the new birth
can even in its individual life manifest a greater extent of development. The worldly ego raises itself in the course of generations. The
majority of men however remain inert. Their aim is only to flee from
suffering, but it is suffering which alone is still capable of frightening us from that inertia which would change every sphere to a swamp.
They seek to escape pain; they do not seek escape from the depths.

There is a limit to ethics, and though conscience, duty, and morality pave the way for the true blending of all human beings, *even
the loftiest morality will not lead us above worldliness,* and its all-interwoven cosmic life needs good and bad as little as does the Godhead
in which it is perfected. The Godhead is perfection of good and bad:
it does nothing but love. Morality is a function—the highest—of the
separate self, but it does not suffice for our cosmic, metaphysical mission. God is no Philistine. He is the blissful wayfarer, the creative rev-

olutionary, the Lord of every possibility, which for ever excludes all impossibilities.

Divine journeying is never-ending creative life and perpetual youth and renewal; it is heroism and love, raging whirlwind and profoundest calm. And there nothing can be lost, everything is forever preserved in the seraphic at-oneness of God. But if the ego rest in sluggish fear, then stress and fear is intensified throughout totality; while if we journey, all stress and fear vanishes like in a fleeting moment.

Thou Nature Beneath Me

We are moving beyond Nature! This is the impetus of our time. From *Nature* has come *World*; and the cause of all Nature and Nature's riddles is this: the womb of Nature is in labor to bring forth World. Human history has been the struggle of Man with Nature. And we are still so bewildered by being caught in the spell of Nature that we think of Nature as the All. Common sense thinks that there is nothing beyond Nature, that everything is accomplished *in the course of Nature*, and that all which does not fit into this framework is unscientific phantasy. We ourselves are seen as an appendage of Nature, lifted for a moment above it, but entirely subject to it. This however is only an attempt to save in theory something which in reality has already been lost. *We ourselves are the actual breaking-out of the natural.* We are nature-subjugators and nature-liberators. *World* is completely humanized *Nature*, as *Pleroma* will be deified *World*. Nature is not the All: she is the deepest abyss of the divine All. Natural laws are not eternal: they make way for World-laws, and these again make way for the heavenly order. Nature-manifestation is but the way we—germinating in Nature—have travelled.

The zenith of the World, into which we are entering today, has made us greater than Nature, just as now we shall grow above World. Nature is now less than we are. Our supra-personal task is no longer that realm but the kingdom of Heaven, not the forming of the World but its fruition and liberation. And so to Nature I say: "Thou," for without me—the human—she would not exist. If I wrenched myself out of Nature she would sink into nothingness. "Thou, Nature" says that Nature is myself, albeit in the stifling prism of matter and death-manifestations.

Physical matter is a nothing, and it is just the most exact physics which has demonstrated the nothingness of the material. Nature is the grave of God; the World is His resurrection; Pleroma is His ascent to Heaven. Nature and all her creative mechanism is unthinkable without divine origin; it is divine perfection which has descended into her, into the chaos of the abyss. The reason for Nature's ascent is that we are hidden in Nature as her kernel for the sake of her development and unfolding. And this development is ceaselessly breaking up all "naturalness." That which "natures" in Nature, the mechanical, the material frees itself in "World", in humanity. Nature is continually overcome and disintegrated. All higher shaping of her is humanizing, is becoming World, a return to the Godhead.

More and more must we wean ourselves from the materialistic delusion that Nature, the suns and stars, the earth could have existed without us and before us. If we go back to the more primitive in the scale of living beings, we find there no experience of stars, geological epochs, chemical compounds or electrical processes. Only through living beings has all this come forth from the chaotic primeval basis. There was never a ready-made organic nature in this form before any beings took cognizance. The development of inorganic nature runs parallel with the ascent of living beings to *human* beings. If the organization of our mind should alter in the least, if our mission were in the most minute degree other than it is, the firmest laws of physics and the courses of the stars would collapse. But the fashioning of Nature is not wholly or solely our work. In everything remains a residue which is not formed by us—just that which is pure Nature, the Nature-abyss. The earth today, the stars running in their circuits, the past of the geologic epochs, *is all our human experience,* all our human need, all our becoming human. That which in the forming is matter and mechanism belongs to Nature. But that which—though still attached to the depths—is ascent, is sense and beauty, *this comes from us;* this is the resurrection that comes from returning home and defies mechanical explanation.

The pure state of Nature is, like pure perfection, a limit state. It cannot exist a single moment without ascending and bringing a World into being. And then too, the Nature-realm is not sharply divided from World and Pleroma like the floors of a house. They are total life-conditions of the divine soaring, and the Nature-condition is completely absorbed in World-existence, as World-existence is dissolved in heavenly perfection. Therefore we cannot divide the mechanical sharply from supra-mechanical. As, after mixing two colors, we cannot separate what comes from each of them, so we cannot easily tear apart the mechanical and the living in their mutual interpenetration. We shall limit the domain of Nature-investigation to that which comes from the mechanical and the material. Two things must be the foundation of all natural science of the future: *Nature is only a part of the totality*, only the material rigidity based on death; *mechanical nature-investigation does not even give a complete picture of the nature-abyss*, but merely the relation of parts of Nature to one another.

Natural science has added a theory to exact mechanical investigation—materialism. The eye of the man of science today *is blinded to an incredible degree to every fact which might contradict this theory*, and this in itself indicates that materialism is by no means only a theory that has been carried to excess, but a formative power. It has been shown that matter, stuff, is but an abstraction, not a fact of experience. Yet just for this reason matter and materialism are not merely perverted theory, but a deathward-directed demonical cleaving to nothing; that is why matter appears so concrete and so real in the same way that nothingness and death and appearance are realities. We wanted to limit ourselves to the description of the mechanical basis of the natural—and instead of the materialistic explanation fettering the natural phenomenon to death, we wished by living experience to participate in the liberating explanation of Nature. A small step in this direction is made if exact investigation proceeds to eliminate the idea of matter and substance; but this is far from the last step: the *conception of force must go too*.

Nature is becoming an organ of the higher realms. The mechanical too appears to us mechanical when we consider it from within, subjected to its constraint. In its entirety it is guidance fused in seraphic fire and born in depths of superhuman wisdom. And also *that* part in this mechanical nature *which is ascent,* does not come from Nature but from us, from our growth and our present condition.

The various natural sciences are clearly differentiated from one another in regard to the position, which they each occupy vis-à-vis mathematics. Present-day naturalism takes physics to be the basic science—chemistry being considered as a special branch of it. But we cannot maintain this conception for it rests on the doctrine of the *unity of Nature.* To us Nature is no unity, she is actually a multiplicity of disconnected things. All things which are material and separated cannot be interlaced; they can only be alongside of each other being brought into union by a higher arrangement above them. Nature is the divine in a broken-up state. When, supra-personally, in sidereal birth, we rise above World and above death, we find unity, not in the depths but in the heights of the divine.

The further we rise above Nature the less can there be a single all-embracing natural science. It is true that physics, chemistry and biology form a unit as a three-membered organism, but they are beginning to separate from each other more distinctly; *it becomes impossible to reduce chemistry and biology to physics.* These three basic types of nature-knowledge form a ring with three poles, and it depends upon the state of the world from which side we approach this ring. Up to the present, physics seemed to be the first—the most basic—of these three sciences, because physics is knowledge from the point of view of pressure and push and spatial motion. Physics is the way of looking at things by the *hylic* mind, being imprisoned in the material, knowing only "hate-divided" things, and the palpability of pressure and push. But with an overpowering impulse we want to advance beyond corporeality.

The Seven Pillars of the World

The World rests on seven pillars, on seven directions of action of the divine vibration. *Death* is one pole, and all that belongs to its realm—the sense-limitation, the feeding-plane, the worthless-mechanical and the kingdom of the body. *The anti-pole is God*—the Lord of abundance and completion and bliss. Above death rises consciousness, which sets free, and higher still the ego. Consciousness, freedom and harmony lead to God. Where there is death, consciousness, ego, freedom and harmony there lies the realm of valuation and revaluation. *Here is the place where the pillars of the world become the wings of the world,* where, by our deeds we can give wings to the world. But before we can see how death and knowledge, ego, harmony and freedom are in perpetual revaluation, how they separate and mutually exchange their missions, we must look at the innermost core of *death*—suffering.

Suffering is the great touchstone to all conceptions of the world and to all religions—for none escapes the question "Why suffering?" Suffering seems the completely meaningless, without a place in the glorious Godhead of infinite meaning. However, this is but the corollary of a quite personal way of looking at things. Only to the suprapersonal view is contradiction made plain. What is frightful to the narrowness of personal life is not so to the supra-personal life. We must look at suffering as threefold: as a driving desire to create, an illusion and a goad. Thus suffering is the meaning of the world. The

more we are stuck fast in the hylic, the more we feel only bodily pleasure as positive. Yet the highest bodily pleasure is for the soul only
deepest disgust, and the highest joy of the soul—its ecstatic stream-
ing forth—is to the body only a painful death.

The common man is by no means the primitive man; he rather
represents the world, the world midways. Deep down in the world
of unfreedom, as in the heights of perfection, there are no conflicts.
Between the heights and the depths is the realm of the great tasks
and the goad of evil. These contradictions of life are not more sur-
prising than the contradictions of the intellect and the friction of
matter. High above world, above intellect and matter, there, in the
At-Oneness can we expect a solution. Yet we must never forget that
the great question is not "Is life enjoyable?" but solely "Is the world
fulfilling its divine mission?"

Without the goad of necessity the world would stagnate.
Worldly life is born again and again in deadly necessity. *Everything
worldly is only an organ of the higher.* But *thing* and *person* hinder
us from beholding the higher. Above them do we behold it, where
all physical pain has ended, because we have outgrown their constric-
tion. Nowhere does the Godhead reveal itself more divinely than in
the compulsion of suffering, which is the highest of all compulsions.
Even the best of us scarcely begin to apprehend the Godhead in
freedom. Only through extreme necessity have we risen to the height
of the present. It is not accidental that we place the full development
of the human germ out of the abyss of nature in the great need of the
glacial epoch, this divine chisel. Without suffering man would remain
in the vegetating existence, and many would feel comfortable there.

It is not evil so much as inertia that we find abominable. The
meaning of the world is not the elimination of conflicts, but the annihilation of *nothingness*, of the unimportant, the immature. There
is then for us scarcely a more glorious certainty than that Divinity
must come. With iron necessity the impetus of need forces everything
down into the purgatory of purification till it is matured. No matter
how superhuman the claims of Divinity, we know they will be met,
for *there will come a driving compulsion more powerful than any yet.*
The compulsion of exhaustion and of the end, the compulsion of
suffocation in the swamp will teach men that *they do not need ego-*

ism, being and matter. Ascent achieved through holy necessity is the meaning of the world.

The coarsest form of suffering is bodily pain and illness. It is as if the world-pressure were forcing itself in from without; and the overwhelmed person cannot defend himself. When an ego is ready for higher existence and yet remains still in the depths, it lies exposed and vulnerable, for only from the heights are the depths directed and guided. Illness means that the conflicts, frictions and imperfections of the material merge into the person. Among lower organisms, animals and plants, even among primitive human beings, we find few illnesses, for the infallible spirit of the species prevents injuries better than our erring egos. In man, therefore, illness may be looked at as a fault, for if man were on the level where he belongs, if he were a well-functioning organ of the All as he was intended to be, he would change his course and travel in freedom towards the higher spheres, and *such a man could not fall ill*. The perfect man, he who is journeying to the heights, stands above illness. We can, then, overcome illness, although it is often too late for this. Moreover, there are faults and illnesses which are so generally human that in practice no human being escapes them. *How* each one falls ill is as characteristic for him as is his face.

We must discount the materialistic physiological explanation which accounts for illnesses only by disturbances, damages, bacilli. Such disturbances are so overwhelming in the material that no living body is immune to them. If the body nevertheless lives, it is solely because it is guided by something higher. Hence vital health is as much a gift of the higher spirit within, as illness is a fault, and so much the more the higher a man has risen. It is *not nature that cures* but only the higher self. Nature can do *nothing but open wounds*. Therefore, all "natural" methods are a return to that which lies beneath us, and there is no reason we should not use the means science has placed in our hands. The words "poison" and "knife" do not frighten us. Yet we cannot believe that surgery or other medical methods can *by themselves* accomplish much. It is significant that these methods serve us best in cases of external injuries or wounds and prove less useful the more we approach the constitutional illnesses. Disease is not of a material and physiological but of a metaphysical nature. When the body falls ill, the whole self has first been shaken in its depths and can in consequence not protect the body from material attacks. *Disease is not only a bodily process but a disturbance of the totality.*

There is no such thing as mental disease. What we call mental disease is the disturbance of the connections which exist between the mind and the material life. Even in the most frantic mental disturbances *the personality is preserved.* Instead, these diseases are often nothing but intensifications of qualities that already existed in the person. All "madness" is an extreme disregard and overleaping of actual realities.

Suffering belongs to the kingdom of death. Above death consciousness has risen as the first liberation of all that is dead, and further, the ego, which is the basis for all supra-personal action. And we found the realm of valuation to be the great return of the meaningless-mechanical to the purposeful-meaningful. Here we discovered that the divine cycle is not a perpetual repetition of the same thing, it is creative renovation on the seraphic plane.

Freedom however leads us ever yet nearer to the anti-pole of death; the pole of highest vitality. Freedom is the preliminary stage to the highest level; it is the innermost essence of activity and vitality; it is not only absence of compulsion, but something positive. For the sake of freedom God has manifested Himself in the world. Man is this realm of freedom, the realm of free choice above all vacillation and meaningless strife. Man is the divine strife in God. Thus man stands between compulsion and freedom, coming from perpetual compulsion and going toward freedom. The *wholly* free is the Godhead that follows only its own law, its own compulsion. In the Godhead compulsion and freedom coincide. He who denies the *freedom of will and action* denies willing and acting altogether, and therewith denies the existence of man. In man is completed the advance from necessity to freedom, the most primal attribute of humanity. I am free when I act according to my own inner law. Such a compulsion from my inner self does not make my self unfree. In this sense freedom means the growth of humanity above the compulsion of nature. The law of humanity has become stronger than the mechanical law of things. The compulsory law of death cannot be arbi-

trarily broken in particular cases, only—an unheard-of greater and
profounder marvel—be overcome as a whole, in the higher spheres.
And *will* is not something free or unfree, it is the expression for that
which *has become* free, the consequence of freedom.

The transvaluation of all life by sidereal birth is also noticeable
in the Arts. Hitherto, the Arts have striven to give—in picture and
poetry—a sort of copy of higher ideal realities. The picturing of such
ideal realms is the expression of our remoteness from Divinity. But
we have outlived even the most blissful regions that we can picture.

Instead of the absolute known, there is a hiddenness which can
only be ended by deeds, and not by knowledge gained by manipula-
tions. Godhead is the eternally unknown, before which the known
perishes, according to the word of God: "Man may not see me and
live." Never can Godhead be unveiled; it must be gained by faith,
which is stronger than all contradictions. *Doubt*, if it does not lead
to belief is the primal treachery.

We have seen that the divine cycle is but perpetual sidereal
birth, perpetual soaring above and embracing the fulness that arises
from the eternal-only-once. And *this sidereal birth of all totality*,
incessantly rejuvenating and raising every individuality from within,
is the highest we can experience. God is not the refuge of the
weak, but overflowing energy and action, the highest plane in which
all rests, for *without the highest nothing can exist*. Godhead is the
final explanation of all things and all happenings in Nature, World
and Pleroma.

Now, as the world becomes too narrow for us, we are longing
for such super-human action. We need now *world-dissolution, world-
liberation, world-formation*. But weak as we are, we would never by
ourselves bring this about. Faced with the great question "what shall
we do?", humanity is helpless. *Yet*, if in seraphic fire we expand ourselves supra-personally, then we gain the strength for all-embracing
action. *Everything is possible if we act in the spirit of the Divine*. It
is possible for us to journey endlessly and yet to be at rest, possible
for us to rise above death and to gain blessedness. The price at which
we grow is *death*. We must first *un-thing* and *un-I* ourselves. It is not
my little ego which must perform the unheard of; I can only bring it

about when I go through death, when my ego expands to the All, when I rise to the eternal impetuosity of divine action.

In the Creation God acted before me and without me. Now God draws me into His creative power and acts through me and with me. In partaking in world-liberation and world-formation do I become myself, a living being. I take the whole creation in my arms and bring it to the Godhead. Thus the pillars of the world become wings. Man goes through death, hurling himself in ecstatic bliss into God. Death, the "I am not" is the highest deed of humanity, as the "I" was the highest aim of nature.

But we do not mean *the death of extinction*, the dark death which we, trembling, fear and flee. The overcoming of this death, the victory over the end is indeed the glorious crowning of all action, the fundamental impulse of all our efforts. When I expand myself to the All, I escape death. Death is not at the end of life, it is always amidst life. What has become "I" has a share in all totality. I am flowing through the whole divine soaring, as in worldly life the whole is flowing through me. My death is my life in divine outpouring. I no longer *have* myself, I pour out myself in overflowing giving. And when I have gone through this death, infinity can nevermore hurl me back into worldly life. Death is nothing but body-death, death of limitation. The dead cling to God who takes them up in tender embrace; and in God, in my seraphic pouring through everything—not in the narrowness of my person—lies the absolute guarantee of my immortality.

But this divine death cannot be compared with sleep. *Sleep* is an expression of the finiteness of our material consciousness; it is a transitory death for the sake of transitory renewal. The new form of life is not sleep, but the highest ascent of the soul. That which was invisible and insignificant in our worldly life, due to the narrowness of our person, has now become an organ of God. In the Godhead, everything lives in the omnipresent. Here, outside the Godhead, we live in the present too, but it is a present that is like a point and incessantly eludes us. And we live in time, which consists of the past, which no longer is, and of the future, which is not yet, both separated by this elusive point. But in God's all-embracing love and wisdom, past and present are one in an unheard-of living present. Everything is preserved there that has ever escaped the lower death. And this only we desire, that all which ever had to meet such death, shall rise above that terror. Everything, whatever it may be, heaven and earth and splendor and we ourselves, shall become expressions of the divine soaring. *Nothing shall be any longer by itself, but all shall be in God's possession.* Height and depth, man and nature and completion attain their highest meaning in God-community.

The star-like urge drives us ever further, and though we have to leave everything—*the whole of the cycle is highest glory.* The divine oscillation is but an inconceivable exaltation. What is the most exalted is the truest. Godhead is the storm-breath of beauty and infinity, making everything perish and everything germinate, the divine-creating-above-itself. The most transcendent embrace of the fervor of love is for us like being crushed. Before this highest embodiment of love the I can no longer exist. What can the petty raptures of life mean for us, who, in sacred poverty, hover now above life and immerse in bliss?

The Consecration of the Deed

Now we will stand sponsor to the deed. What must we do to begin sidereal birth? *Transcendent joy we must do!* Never was a doctrine announced which was easier to fulfill: *first we must rejoice!* Rejoice at the crushing love which will enter into us, rejoice at our endless journeying, rejoice that we shall expand into the boundless regions. The transcendent joy is participation in the blissful divine soaring. But how can we achieve the tremendous act which takes the breath away, if we do not first rejoice? That would be as saying to the dumb: "Sing!" or to the cripple: "Defend yourself!" Without the supramundane joy there would be nothing but powerless, tortured asceticism. Yet we do not want to torture, but to heal, and, in freedom, to act. The Godhead does not restrict but fortifies life. Hence the transcendent exaltation is the *consecration of action*. No one can be in holy poverty if he only reduces himself to privation without gaining something new. I cannot tear myself from my foundations unless the exaltation of the higher has filled me.

No one who has followed us so far will believe that we have been preaching enjoyment and pleasure as the highest. Holy poverty and its supra-personal love-deed are polar opposites of mere pleasure, pleasure-seeking. Enjoyment of pleasure was necessary in the period of ego-formation, but in world-decline it is downright wantonness. World-decline is freeing the ego, the little "I," which must never rest in enjoyment and seek to live on in worldly fashion. That would be death indeed. Divine Joy is not a comfort that makes the world-house habitable for us; it is a bursting delight and the consecration of *action* and not of death.

We shall not be freed from want and distress; they prepare us to achieve the supra-mundane deed. No paradise can satisfy us. The sidereal strength in me is my paradise, only the consecration of the joy is my infinite mission. The power of the sidereal birth now takes the place of the forces of nature, which will only come into being, when the power of race, body, instincts and nature's depths is exhausted. This synthesis of World, God and Deed is the meaning of the present. And with the transcendental joy begin the new sidereal experiences. Suddenly we have the unparalleled realization that *we need not despair*. This baptism of exaltation is not sect nor party, but something which *all* can embrace, without distinction.

We have sought here to trace out the two main, polar trends— *the liberating germination,* arising from the seraphic new birth, and the *forming condensation,* down to the death-zero-point. Within myself I feel this stirring, divided and yet absolutely One. *Within myself is this suffocation, even to death, and to the new boundless germination.* And we have wished *not only to indicate this way, but to travel along it.* Yet, to give oneself up to these contrary positions within us can only be the task of generations. The springing up in us of the urge to act in totality, to embrace the All, is nothing but the Deed itself, beyond all words. Now there is nothing but one ardent embrace—and with outstretched arms and overwhelming exaltation I pour myself out in the fires of sidereal birth, starlike above all stars.

Index

Index

235